Lift Every Voice

A volume in
Urban Education Studies Series
Nicholas D. Hartlep and Thandeka K. Chapman, *Series Editors*

Urban Education Studies Series

Nicholas D. Hartlep and Thandeka K. Chapman, *Series Editors*

Black Males Matter: A Blueprint for Creating School and Classroom Environments to Support Their Academic and Social Development—A Sourcebook (2021)
    Cherrel Miller Dyce, Julius Davis, and Shadonna Gunn

Through the Fog: Towards Inclusive Anti-Racist Teaching (2019)
    Tara L. Affolter

Better Teachers, Better Schools: What Star Teachers Know, Believe, and Do (2017)
    Valerie Hill-Jackson and Delia Stafford

Colluding, Colliding, and Contending with Norms of Whiteness (2016)
    Jennifer L. S. Chandler

Better Principals, Better Schools: What Star Principals Know, Believe, and Do (2015)
    Delia Stafford and Valerie Hill-Jackson

Intersectionality and Urban Education: Identities, Policies, Spaces & Power (2014)
    Carl A. Grant and Elisabeth Zwier

Lift Every Voice

Radford University Teacher Education Students

edited by

Antonio L. Ellis
American University

Lisa Maria Grillo
Howard University

Jania Hutchinson
Radford University

INFORMATION AGE PUBLISHING, INC.
Charlotte, NC • www.infoagepub.com

Library of Congress Cataloging-in-Publication Data

A CIP record for this book is available from the Library of Congress
http://www.loc.gov

ISBN: 979-8-88730-753-4 (Paperback)
       979-8-88730-754-1 (Hardcover)
       979-8-88730-755-8 (E-Book)

Copyright © 2024 Information Age Publishing Inc.

All rights reserved. No part of this publication may be reproduced, stored in a retrieval system, or transmitted, in any form or by any means, electronic, mechanical, photocopying, microfilming, recording or otherwise, without written permission from the publisher.

Printed in the United States of America

This book is dedicated to Dr. Elizabeth "Liz" Altieri for your extensive contributions to educational research and practice.

Happy Retirement (May 2024)

CONTENTS

Foreword ix
William Bill Ayers

Preface xi

Acknowledgments xv

1 Harmonies and Melodies 1
  Victoria Branscome

2 Observing an Amazing Second-Grade Class 7
  Claire Morris

3 Identifying Influential Teachers From a Student's Perspective 13
  Shyheim Woods

4 Educators Promoting Growth Beyond Standardized Test Scores 19
  Kaylee Golder

5 Dr. Stirling Barfield: An Instant Role Model 25
  Madison F. Keaton

6 Mrs. Leona K. Brown: What an Extraordinary Teacher Looks Like 31
  Allison G. Brown

7   How a First Grade Teacher Changed My Life 37
Joleigh Helton

8   Ms. Hart and Mrs. Gilbert: The Inspirations
of a Future Educator 43
Taylor Poff

9   The Impact of an Educator.. 47
Brooke E. Kelly

10 A Teacher of Love, Compassion, and an Influence 53
Christian R. Worley

11 What Is a Quality Teacher? Looking Beyond the Intellectual 59
Maddison Parrish

12 Inspired by an African American Male English Teacher 65
Jabin Walker

13 Overcoming the Hardships of My Early Education 67
Katherine L. Wagoner

14 A Teacher's Encouragement Led Me to College 71
Jada Turner

15 The Effect a Good Teacher Has on Students 75
Jenna Staton

16 The Presence of Ms. Miller: Teacher as a Caregiver........................ 81
Britney Conner

17 How Teachers Have Affected Me 85
Jacob Mays

18 Mrs. Owens and Ms. C: A Comparative Analysis of Two Teachers .. 89
Kelcie Lemons

Afterword: Embracing the Power of Student Voices
in Teacher Education 93
Antonio L. Ellis

About the Editors 95

About the Contributors.. 97

FOREWORD

Students who are just now becoming teachers come to teaching with a heavy set of ready-made stereotypes awaiting them: the lazy, incompetent teacher protected by his self-interested union eating snacks and reading the newspaper at his desk in the front of the room while the kids run wild; the unmotivated bureaucrat who goes through the motions, takes attendance, passes out the work sheets, and collects her steady paycheck while her disconnected students doze off in boredom; the solitary teacher-hero fighting valiantly to save the good kids from their terrible families, rotten neighborhoods, deplorable peers, and overburdened schools. These cliches and conventional images are more than unhelpful—they shape expectations and become part of the larger meta-narrative that is disempowering and deskilling teachers, reducing them to clerks and auditors rather than the relationship-builders and agents of enlightenment, liberation, and transformation that they aspire (and work hard every day) to be.

These are troubling times for teachers, to be sure: powerful and noisy forces marching under the banner of "reform" conceive of education as a product to be bought and sold at the marketplace, promote privatizing one aspect after another of a school's vital functions, and frame teachers as assembly line workers pouring knowledge into the upturned heads of passive students as they bump along the K–12 conveyor belt called school. The deeper design of the "reformers" has become crystal clear: they are determined to devour public education altogether.

There is, however, a more hopeful and helpful truth within reach: children and youth know who cares for them, who values them, who challenges and nourishes them, builds meaningful relationships with them, and takes their side. Students value good teachers, and parents do too. Teaching is hard daily work that draws on a person's deepest intelligences as well as unfathomable reserves of energy, a daily grind that is excruciatingly complex, filled with discovery and surprise, improvisation and invention, creativity and imagination, joy and also frustration. Teachers experience profound challenges and periods of loneliness; they can also feel discouraged some of the time and over their heads much of the time—this is when teachers have to dig deep within themselves, and outside themselves, as well, to fellow teachers, parents, and students, in order to regroup and rise up stronger.

Lift Every Voice is a gift for teachers who want to dig deep and grow their teaching souls. With this volume Antonio L. Ellis, Lisa Maria Grillo, and Jania Hutchinson gather together the perspectives of students of teaching who offer unique insights into the trembling reality of actual teaching—the intellectual demand, the ethical purpose, moral meaning, and the larger spirit, that is, a sense of the soul of teaching. It is this territory—teaching as a relentlessly moral endeavor, teaching as ethical action, messy, grand, and tangled—that cries out urgently to be explored.

These sparks of meaning-making energy are on a voyage into teaching, and they resist the scholarly literature in which teachers are dissected and measured, talked about but rarely listened to, and their performances set against student outcomes—"scientized" teaching, and teachers as data. As the men with the megaphones shout about "data-driven teaching," these authors stay true to a different ideal: teaching that is data-informed but student-driven. They are knowledgeable about research and sophisticated about facts and figures without falling into data's arid and dreary thrall.

The disability rights movement is guided by a moral principle that applies here: Nothing About Us Without Us! In other words, the people with the problems or challenges are also the people with the solutions.

Praise to Antonio L. Ellis, Lisa Maria Grillo, and Jania Hutchinson for bringing that principle to life in teaching and teacher education.

— **William Bill Ayers**

PREFACE

As editors of *Lift Every Voice: Radford University Teacher Education Students*, it is with great pride and humility that we introduce this collection of narratives, insights, and reflections. This book represents a groundbreaking effort to amplify the voices and life experiences of undergraduate teacher education students at Radford University. Through their narratives, these students emerge as authorities on the subject of teacher education, challenging traditional hierarchies of knowledge and expertise. At the heart of this volume lies a commitment to centering student voices in the conversation about teacher preparation. Too often, the perspectives of those most directly impacted by educational practices are overlooked or marginalized. *Lift Every Voice* seeks to rectify this by providing a platform for undergraduate teacher education students to share their stories, insights, and critiques.

The critical storytelling methodology employed by our contributors serves as a powerful tool for illuminating the ways in which classroom practices impact students academically, socially, and emotionally. By weaving together personal anecdotes, reflections, and analyses, these students offer a nuanced and multifaceted understanding of the teacher-student dynamic. As editors, our hope is that the stories, anecdotes, and analysis contained within this volume will be valuable to preservice and classroom teachers alike. Whether navigating the complexities of classroom management, grappling with issues of diversity and inclusion, or reflecting on the emotional dimensions of teaching and learning, the insights shared by our student contributors offer invaluable guidance and inspiration.

Lift Every Voice serves as a testament to the resilience, agency, and creativity of undergraduate teacher education students. Despite facing numerous challenges and obstacles, these students demonstrate a remarkable capacity to learn, grow, and thrive in the face of adversity. Their stories serve as a source of inspiration and empowerment for educators at all stages of their careers. Lessons we hope readers will take away from this volume include:

The Importance of Student Perspectives: One key takeaway from this book is the recognition of the importance of centering student perspectives in discussions about teacher education. By legitimizing the voices and life experiences of Radford University undergraduate teacher education students, we aim to challenge traditional hierarchies of knowledge and expertise and highlight the valuable insights that students bring to the field of education.

The Power of Critical Storytelling: Through the critical storytelling methodology employed by our contributors, readers gain a deeper understanding of the ways in which classroom practices impact students academically, socially, and emotionally. By sharing personal anecdotes, reflections, and analyses, our student authors illuminate the complexities of the teacher-student dynamic and offer valuable insights into the challenges and opportunities inherent in the field of teacher education.

The Resilience and Agency of Students: Another important lesson from this book is the resilience and agency demonstrated by undergraduate teacher education students at Radford University. Despite facing numerous challenges and obstacles, these students demonstrate a remarkable capacity to learn, grow, and thrive in the face of adversity. Their stories serve as a source of inspiration and empowerment for educators at all stages of their careers.

The Value of Diversity and Inclusion in Education: The narratives shared in this book highlight the importance of diversity and inclusion in education. By centering the experiences of students from diverse backgrounds, we aim to promote greater understanding and appreciation of the rich tapestry of human experiences within educational settings. This emphasis on diversity and inclusion is essential for creating more equitable and inclusive learning environments for all students.

The Potential for Positive Change: Ultimately, we hope that this book will inspire readers to reflect critically on their own practices and assumptions as educators. By engaging with the stories, anecdotes, and analyses presented in this volume, readers have the opportunity to gain new perspectives, challenge conventional wisdom, and envision innovative approaches to teacher education. We believe that by lifting every voice and embracing the insights of undergraduate teacher education students, we can work together to create a more just, equitable, and inclusive education system for all learners.

We extend our deepest gratitude to the student contributors for their courage, vulnerability, and authenticity in sharing their stories. We also thank our readers for engaging with these narratives with an open mind and heart. May the stories contained within *Lift Every Voice* inspire critical reflection, meaningful dialogue, and positive change within the field of teacher education and beyond. Together, let us lift every voice in the pursuit of a more just, equitable, and inclusive education system for all learners.

ACKNOWLEDGMENTS

To my former Radford University undergraduate students,

Your voices, experiences, and insights have been the guiding light behind this endeavor. As emerging educators, you have demonstrated resilience, compassion, and a deep commitment to the field of teacher education. This book is dedicated to each of you, who have bravely shared your stories and contributed to a richer understanding of the challenges and triumphs encountered in the classroom.

You are the heart and soul of this work, and your willingness to speak truth to power has inspired us all. Your courage in navigating the complexities of teaching and learning has left an indelible mark on our journey together. May your voices continue to echo through the halls of academia, empowering future generations of educators to embrace critical storytelling as a tool for transformation.

With gratitude and admiration,

Professor Antonio L. Ellis

CHAPTER 1

HARMONIES AND MELODIES

Victoria Branscome

Some teachers have consistently succeeded where others continue to fail at teaching students deemed hard to reach, if not unteachable (Ladson-Billings, 1995; Lynn & Jennings, 2009). Some teachers may consider students from my generation, commonly known as Gen Z, as "hard to reach." With this in mind, most of us have encountered one or two teachers with whom we have had love–hate relationships. In my case, it was my middle and high school choir teacher, Mrs. Harmony. Research studies have shown that teacher quality is often considered to be a crucial factor predicting student academic outcomes (Nye et al., 2004; Rivikin et al., 2005). In grade school, I was what you would consider an average student within the general education classroom. In choir, however, I was uniquely gifted. Mrs. Harmony's teaching style was extremely effective for my class's overall performance, but there are several things Mrs. Harmony did that are contrary to best practices for teachers.

For one thing, Mrs. Harmony loved to gossip to anyone who would listen. She had a positive relationship with each of her students—at least, at some point in time. She was also a teacher we could talk to about anything, which was great, except that she transferred private information from one student to another; in other words, she gossiped. Her office was a small closet tucked away in the far corner of the band room. This isolation allowed her to bring students in to talk whenever they needed, without anyone around to hear. After some time in her class, students started to realize that she shared their information to keep the conversation going within those one-on-one sessions. Eventually, only those students who were unashamed of their private information getting out would talk to her.

For a teacher who prided herself on the success of her auditioned groups, she became careless about the selection of its members. The first year she held chamber choir, there were eight students, one for each split voice part. The next year, there were 16, two for each. However, during my last 2 years in chamber choir, there were at least 25 students. A once-exclusive class had become available for half of the students who auditioned. This became an obstacle for Mrs. Harmony every time the group had an opportunity to perform.

In the early days, it seemed like every other week the chamber choir went on field trips to perform in town. This was a great experience for those who were planning to pursue the music field. And with eight people (mostly juniors and seniors), it was easy for all of us to travel in two cars. However, carpooling was out of the question with a class of 25. That size group required a school bus and extra planning, which greatly limited the places we could perform. With eight people, we performed for the police department, nursing homes, offices in the courthouse, and schools throughout the county, among other places. The larger class was only able to make one special trip, which was to sing for veterans on Veteran's Day. It was a lovely day, but nonetheless, the class simply wasn't as rewarding as it was when class size was smaller.

Another major issue with Mrs. Harmony was that sometimes she behaved like the high school students she taught. For example, many high school students are petty and love arguing. Mrs. Harmony loved to argue back. According to Ellis (2021, p. 3), it is important for teachers to have high expectations for their students. High expectations are not limited to academics only, but also include modeling healthy and desired behaviors. I recall one time when Mrs. Harmony got into an argument with a student in the soprano section. They fought verbally during class, and everyone thought the argument was over at the conclusion of the class session. After class, students filed into the band room to put away their music folders. I was talking to my friend, the girl Mrs. Harmony had argued with, when Mrs. Harmony stormed into the band room, folders in hand, and walked towards Maggie and me. I stepped aside, unsure of what was about to happen, when Mrs. Harmony slammed her music folders and binders down on the floor. It was completely unnecessary in the context of the argument, but Mrs. Harmony wanted to make sure everyone was watching. She got up in Maggie's face, pointed her finger at her, and continued the argument. All the rest of us could do was stand there and watch as Mrs. Harmony argued. The fight eventually ended, and Maggie later complained to members of the school administrative team.

My younger sister is currently a senior in high school and in Mrs. Harmony's class this semester. She was in her class as a freshman but switched electives when COVID-19 commenced, and the chorus was no longer performing. My sister also had several complaints about Mrs. Harmony. She says she has changed and is not like she was previously.

Although Mrs. Harmony was not the best behaved, I still consider her one of my best teachers. She is a uniquely skilled musician and did her job better than most choir directors I've met. She pushed me past my limits and helped me become one of the best singers in the school. She saw potential in me during my early years and gave me every opportunity she could to help me improve. Before I was old enough to participate in chamber choir, on the very first day of school, she invited me to stay after school every day and practice with her exclusive class. I accepted the invitation and when I showed up for practice that afternoon, I realized that I was the only outsider she invited. She helped me and gave me similar opportunities like this throughout the rest of my time in her class.

The most memorable opportunity Mrs. Harmony gave me happened in my senior year.

When I was a freshman, Mrs. Harmony put together a community choir that included choir students from our town and the two surrounding counties. Each school choir practiced music on its own and then gathered for a day to rehearse and perform. For our senior year performance, we convened at Carroll County High. Mrs. Harmony asked her colleague, Dr. Smith, to be the director this particular year, while she chose the musical selections for the concert. Once she got the music, she pulled me aside after class one day and gave me a specific piece of sheet music. She also gave me a slip of paper with a YouTube link on it. She informed me that we would be singing this piece for the Twin-County Chorus, and she wanted me to audition for the alto solo. This was a big deal because the entire song is basically a soprano–alto split solo.

I practiced for over a month before the day of auditions. The director made an announcement before lunch, saying, "If anyone wishes to audition, stay in the auditorium and eat afterwards." Several students from all three schools stayed to audition. He placed us in line by our voice part and had us audition individually in front of everyone. He started with the altos and allowed each student to complete the audition. I was towards the end of the line. After everyone had completed the auditions, I was the only one Dr. Smith asked to remain in the auditorium. I learned it was because I was selected for the alto solo part! The best thing about this scenario is that he had trouble picking the soprano soloist. I was picked as the alto soloist, and now his job was to find the best student to match MY voice. I sang the same two lines of the song repeatedly, until he eventually decided to split the soprano solo between three different sopranos. This opportunity meant a lot to me, because it made me feel that Mrs. Harmony had confidence that I would be selected for the solo. I was the first one chosen, and anyone else who was picked had to match me, not the other way around.

PRACTICAL RECOMMENDATIONS FOR TEACHERS

Based on my personal experiences as a student, as well as my college work studying in the field of education, I now see Mrs. Harmony as an excellent, inspiring teacher—despite a few less desirable quirks. I offer the following recommendations for members of my generation as we take our first steps at the front of the classroom.

First, I contend that best teaching practices begin with having the best beliefs about all students (Ellis, 2021, p. 5). It is important to express your belief in your students' ability to succeed and to provide opportunities for them to soar. You may be the door to a lifetime of success for them.

Second, as schools work to become more personal environments, school administrators will need to help teachers understand their roles as close advisors and mentors to students, while drawing and maintaining clear and obvious boundaries within these relationships (Bernstein-Yamashiro & Noam, 2013). As I have described, Ms. Harmony consistently blurred the lines between student and teacher, sometimes with harmful effects. It is important that teachers remain in their professional, adult role at all times and create boundaries with students.

Third, it is important to remember that teachers and students have grossly unequal power in the classroom. The teacher is the representative of adult authority and is backed up, at least in theory, by the power of force as well as by the tradition of the school (Reinsvold & Cochran, 2012). Avoid getting into power struggles with students. As the adult professional, your role is to model healthy behaviors. Again, although I remember Mrs. Meloni with appreciation, I also remember several unpleasant classroom arguments that should never have occurred.

REFERENCES

Bernstein-Yamashiro, B., & Noam, G. G. (2013). Establishing and maintaining boundaries in teacher–student relationships. *New Directions for Youth Development, 2013*(137), 69–84.

Ellis, A. L. (2021). Mr. Linard H. McCloud: Clarifying excellence in teacher education practice. In A. L. Ellis, N. Bryan, Y. Sealey-Ruiz, I. Toldson, & C. Emdin

(Eds.), *The impact of classroom practices: Teacher educators' reflections on culturally relevant teachers* (pp. 1–6). Information Age Publishing.

Ladson-Billings, G. (1995). Toward a theory of culturally relevant pedagogy. *American Educational Research Journal, 32*(3), 465–491.

Lynn, M., & Jennings, M. E. (2009). Power, politics, and critical race theory: A critical race analysis of a Black male teachers' pedagogy. *Race Ethnicity and Education, 12*(2), 173–196.

Nye, B., Konstantopoulos, S., & Hedges, L. V. (2004). How large are teacher effects? *Educational Evaluation and Policy Analysis, 26*(3), 237–257.

Reinsvold, L. A., & Cochran, K. F. (2012). Power dynamics and questioning in elementary science classrooms. *Journal of Science Teacher Education, 23*(7), 745–768.

Rivikin, S. G., Hanushek, E. A., & Kain, J. F. (2005). Teachers, schools and academic achievement. *Econometrica, 73*(2), 417–458.

CHAPTER 2

OBSERVING AN AMAZING SECOND-GRADE CLASS

Claire Morris

During the 2021 academic year I enrolled in an introduction to education course at Tidewater Community College. I took it as an elective because I wanted to confirm whether I truly wanted to become a teacher or not. While enrolled, I learned that I would be observing a teacher in a classroom for 40 hours. I had never done anything like this before but was excited for the opportunity, because it allowed me to gain first-hand experience in the classroom and better understand what I would encounter as a teacher. I did not realize the knowledge and insight I would gain from this experience.

First, I will describe my classroom observation and mentorship experience. Studies suggest that mentorship in the student teaching internship experience is important, so that interns get not only teaching experience but also support, guidance, and quality feedback that helps them to improve their practice (Del Vecchio & Matsuura, 2016; McGee, 2019). I observed Ms. Tuthill, a lead teacher at B. M. Williams Primary School in Chesapeake, Virginia. That year, she was teaching second grade completely online in an asynchronous format using the Zoom online platform. In my opinion, teaching early childhood classes is challenging, but adding additional obstacles rooted in the COVID-19 pandemic heightened this already challenging work. Educational institutions were one of the sectors most affected by COVID-19 because the teaching and learning process could not be done in the traditional face-to-face format (Azzahra et al., 2022). Ms. Tuthill was also an inclusion teacher. Therefore, children with all types of differing abilities were assigned to her class. Observing an online learning environment and capturing how difficult it was for students to interact with their teacher and their classmates was a new experience for me. At first, I was skeptical about observing online, because I wanted to see a class in person. I was upset because some of my classmates got to observe in person. Nevertheless, with my online instruction experiences, I gained new knowledge about infusing technology in teaching that I probably would not have learned otherwise. To quote my cooperating teacher, "If a teacher can survive teaching through a pandemic, they can survive anything."

Ms. Tuthill quickly adapted to issues that arose while teaching 7- and 8-year-old students stuck in front of a computer screen. It was amazing to witness a teacher delivering instruction to children who did not have foundational knowledge of how to use technology, compounded by differing reading levels. The teacher had been creative with assignments and tools she used for instructional delivery. Most 7- and 8-year-olds are still learning how to spell, read, and write. Amidst the pandemic, having to type on the computer created even more of a challenge for this student population. Ms. Tuthill was patient and found ways to help students through the screen by having them screen-share to defuse some of the technological challenges. She used numerous online techniques, such as screen sharing and using the chat function to communicate with students. Teaching students who are sitting in front of a computer screen with distractions that are beyond the teacher's control can be difficult. In addition to the technology curve, Ms. Tuthill had a mix of children, some of whom had special needs, including diagnoses of autism or attention deficit hyperactivity disorder (ADHD), and who were especially sensitive to distractions and noises. Ms. Tuthill adapted to their needs as well.

Ms. Tuthill displayed not only great patience and understanding, but also an amazing attention to details when supporting her students. Ellis (2021) recommended that teachers consider real-world connections to literature as a viable lesson planning strategy. Ms. Tuthill exemplified this strategy by picking books she knew would pique interest in specific students, such as a book about cats for a reading group with a girl who loved kittens. She also incorporated activities that students found an interest in on their own. An example of this approach was a research project Ms. Tuthill assigned. She showed students how to research various topics and then allowed them to learn and create a project about animals of their choice. She also encouraged students to play interactive educational games during class, such as Kahoot and Blooket.

Ms. Tuthill also used a lot of problem-solving strategies in the virtual classroom while delivering lessons. For example, she guided students through lessons and allowed them to ask questions, as opposed to simply telling them how to do various tasks. Another example was how she encouraged students to practice spelling words themselves, rather than spelling words for them.

Overall, Ms. Tuthill succeeded in creating an environment in her online classroom that allowed students to feel comfortable with learning, which is something I hope to replicate in my own classroom someday. Teachers can create environments that significantly increase the chance for student success. Research on academic and social success has found factors within the school environment to be more significant than factors outside of school, that is, age, sex, social class, and race (Johnston et al., 2019; Lavarin, 2023; MacGregor et al., 1997).

Although I was not with Ms. Tuthill's class every day, I wish I could have been. I saw a lot of myself in Ms. Tuthill. She became a role model for me. She often chatted with me after students logged off, so that she could get to know me more. As Ms. Tuthill reflected, she shared her negative experiences as a student teacher and indicated that she welcomed the opportunity to have student teachers largely because she wanted their experience to be better than her own experience as a student teacher. As a result of our conversations, we discovered that we attended the same high school and had similar experiences and interests in working with children with special needs. After learning these things about Ms. Tuthill, I felt like I had someone to relate and look up to, especially given that she had reached the goal I wanted to obtain in my future career.

Eventually I had an opportunity to go to the school in-person one day when the kids were testing. It was a weird feeling to walk back into an elementary school as an adult in a teachers' role, where students called me Ms. Morris! I loved it. And I enjoyed being at school in-person. During my visit, Ms. Tuthill shared more teaching stories about her teaching career while I helped dismantle her old classroom. She had not been in the classroom physically since prior to the pandemic. She shared stories about working at a disadvantaged school and how she was able to have a positive impact on her students and their families. There was one student, for example, who was in Ms. Tuthill's class the previous year. When he was promoted to the next grade level, his new teacher complained that he was a mischievous student. One day the student reportedly stole from her, which caused the teacher to become very upset. The accusing teacher went to Ms. Tuthill to complain about how awful she felt. During the conversation, Ms. Tuthill asked if she could speak with the student one-on-one. After getting permission, Ms.

Tuthill talked to the student and asked why he felt the need to steal from the teacher. He explained that he and his sister had nothing to eat, and he was going to sell whatever he could to purchase food because his parents could not provide for them. Ms. Tuthill explained that stealing was wrong and gave him some food she had in class and said he could always talk to her when needed. She went back to his teacher and explained the student's rationale for his behavior. Ms. Tuthill also explained that in her experience kids almost never do things out of pure maliciousness; there are usually underlying factors that teachers should take into account so they can provide optimal support for students.

Research studies indicate that high-quality student–teacher relationships are associated with reductions in internalizing and externalizing behaviors in young children, and increased closeness in the student-teacher relationship is associated with decreased student anxiety, improved social skills, and better peer interactions (Nemer et al., 2019). Ms. Tuthill took such an interest in students. As a result, families often invited her to their homes for dinner and other special occasions. Traditionally in the United States, home visits were used as a strategy to address the needs of the children, their families, and their communities (Whyte & Karabon, 2016). Grace and Gerdes (2019) argued that "changing the aim of home visits can provide teachers better insight into the social and cultural ways of knowing that are present in the home and help teachers build positive, trusting relationships with families."

In the neighborhood where most of her students lived, it was not common to see a short blonde White woman casually in the neighborhood. Nevertheless, everyone knew and loved her because of the positive impact she had on students.

Ms. Tuthill also described to me how she loved including the special education (SPED) self-contained class in her inclusion classroom activities. We talked about how we both never had SPED students in our classes when we were students; these students were always isolated from general education classes because of their disabilities. Ms. Tuthill shared that she wanted to make sure general education students understood other children's disabilities and interacted with them, including understanding that some people are blessed with different abilities. During my observation I noticed children in her class were supportive to each other and more accommodating to their peers with autism who needed additional support with various academic and social tasks.

I contend that it is important for children to grow up understanding and embracing diversity and diverse populations. I wish I had gotten this type of exposure earlier in my childhood; however, I did not receive this level of understanding and exposure until I reached adulthood. Ms. Tuthill questioned how the self-contained students might feel if they were included in environments with their general education peers on a regular basis.

My experience with Ms. Tuthill's second-grade class canceled any doubt I had about becoming a teacher. I loved the environment she created in classrooms for students and the inclusive attitude she had towards students with special needs. Her patience, enthusiasm, and attention to detail were truly inspiring. I hope to create a similar educational environment when I become a teacher. She made sure students felt supported, and she encouraged their families to have open communication with her.

Ms. Tuthill is a truly amazing teacher, and I am thankful I got to work with her. Because of my experience in her second-grade class, when people ask me what I want to teach I say, "Hopefully a second or third grade inclusion classroom."

RECOMMENDATIONS FOR PRESERVICE AND INSERVICE TEACHERS

The student practicum experience is an important part of most teacher education programs and is assumed to contribute to student teachers' professional learning (Darling-Hammond, 2010). I recommend more high schools and community colleges consider providing practicum experiences for students who desire to become teachers. Early exposure can help students decide if teaching is a realistic fit for them or not.

A central issue for teacher education is how to foster learning about and from practice *in* practice. Darling-Hammond et al. (2005) argue that clinical experiences should be carefully mentored. During my brief practicum experience, Ms. Tuthill, my cooperating teacher, was very invested in the student teaching experience. However, I did not receive any mentoring or feedback from my community college instructor. I encourage preservice teachers to demand college faculty and cooperating teachers who are committed to providing mentorship and feedback. I contend that theoretical insight from your professor is just as important as practical implications with your cooperating teacher.

REFERENCES

Azzahra, S., Maryanti, R., & Wulandary, V. (2022). Problems faced by elementary school students in the online learning process during the COVID-19 pandemic. *Indonesian Journal of Multidisciplinary Research, 2*(2), 245–256.

Darling-Hammond, L. (2010). Teacher education and the American future. *Journal of Teacher Education, 61*(1–2), 35–47. https://doi.org/10.1177/0022487109348024

Darling-Hammond, L., Hammerness, K., Grossman, P., Rust, F., & Shulman, L. (2005). The design of teacher education programs. In L. Darling-Hammond & J. Bransford (Eds.), *Preparing teachers for a changing world: What teachers should learn and be able to do* (pp. 390–441). Jossey-Bass.

Del Vecchio, M., & Matsuura, M. (2016). Student teacher observation: Perspectives on evaluation and criteria. *Studies in International Relations, 37*(1), 53–72.

Ellis, A. L. (2021). Motivation and its relationship to reading achievement for two middle school African American males. *Journal of African American Males in Education (JAAME), 12*(1), 16–34.

Grace, M., & Gerdes, A. C. (2019). Parent-teacher relationships and parental involvement in education in Latino families. *Contemporary School Psychology, 23*, 444–454.

Johnston, C. B., Herzog, T. K., Hill-Chapman, C. R., Siney, C., & Fergusson, A. (2019). Creating positive learning environments in early childhood using teacher-generated prosocial lessons. *Journal of Educational Research and Practice, 9*(1), 10.

Lavarin, M. A. (2023). Let the schoolhouse say, Amen: The pedagogical congruency between the Black church and critical literacy. In S.A. Robinson & A.L. Ellis (Eds.), *Critical literacy and its impact on Black boys' reading readiness.* (pp. 1–16). Information Age Publishing.

MacGregor, R. R., Nelson, J. R., & Wesch, D. (1997). Creating positive learning environments: The school-wide student management program. *Professional School Counseling, 1*(2), 33–35.

McGee, I. E. (2019). Developing mentor teachers to support student teacher candidates. *Southeast Regional Association of Teacher Educators (SRATE) Journal, 28*(1), 23–30.

Nemer, S. L., Sutherland, K. S., Chow, J. C., & Kunemund, R. L. (2019). A systematic literature review identifying dimensions of teacher attributions for challenging student behavior. *Education and Treatment of Children, 42*(4), 557–578.

Whyte, K. L., & Karabon, A. (2016). Transforming teacher–family relationships: Shifting roles and perceptions of home visits through the funds of knowledge approach. *Early Years, 36*(2), 7–221.

CHAPTER 3

IDENTIFYING INFLUENTIAL TEACHERS FROM A STUDENT'S PERSPECTIVE

Shyheim Woods

An influential educator is one who inspires students and grants them opportunities to realize their self-worth. These educators are individuals who awaken students to new possibilities by allowing them to transcend their experiences and limitations (Darling-Hammond, 2006). Primary school educators are passionate and adamant about exposing students to the possibilities of higher education. They often leave impressions on students in exceptionally positive ways (Broughton, 2019). There are many influential educators in K–12 schools; however, not all teachers impact their students in positive ways. According to Delpit (2012), as cited in Broughton (2019), "'Warm demanders' are the educators who would expect a great deal of their students, convince them of their own brilliance and help them to reach their potential in a disciplined and structured environment" (p. 9). Unfortunately, not all educators possess these qualities, standards, and expectations. In unique ways, educators who lack positive characteristics and professionalism are just as important as their counterparts on the opposite end of the spectrum.

This chapter is largely focused on previous high school and college educators who have both positively and negatively impacted me, and how these educators have impacted my life's trajectory. I entered Bassett High School in Bassett, Virginia, in August 2017, as a teenager with a few friends. My grade point average (GPA) was 4.0, and I had completed middle school with extraordinary grades. I got great scores on my Virginia State Standards of Learning (SOL) standardized tests, and everything was going well.

Upon entering high school, I noticed many changes within myself, and I became less motivated in school. I began associating with mischievous students who shared classes with me, while avoiding my original friends. The feeling of detachment and impassiveness began to appear more as the number of my absences grew, causing my academic performance to decline. My teachers, for the most part, did nothing to support me or identify why I lacked motivation. My mother tried her best to intervene. I intentionally avoided talking about school with my family and friends. I saw a bleak future for myself and concluded that no one cared about my well-being. At this point, I did not think I would graduate or accomplish much during my high-school years, which was typical for my family. My bad habits remained constant through my freshman year and continued when I became a sophomore. However, my habits were quickly altered when I was introduced to several inspiring teachers.

Before entering my sophomore year of high school, I registered for an art course and a Spanish course. I did not see myself succeeding in Spanish, especially since I struggled with the content, but I felt confident with art. The instructors of these classes, Ms. Valerie Clarke and Ms. Mercedes Fleagle, were the first teachers who compelled me to do better in school. They changed my attitude toward school and unintentionally helped me gain the motivation I needed to succeed. This became even more prominent after my father's death. On October 7, 2018, my father, Conrad (CJ) Prunty, died in a car accident. After his death, I once again became unmotivated to attend school, but this time my teachers, especially Ms. Clarke and Ms. Fleagle, provided support. From what I recall, these teachers informed my classmates of the incident, used their class time to make cards for my family, and sent text messages and emails to me regarding my loss. Several classmates provided comfort by disclosing their losses. Upon my return to school, Ms. Clarke embraced me with a gentle hug.

This experience changed my perspective on teachers and still affects me today. I once believed that educators solely focused on academic work; however, the kindness and empathy displayed by these teachers debunked my previous assumptions. I now had a reason to make these teachers proud, to do better in school and rise to their expectations.

Moreover, teachers like my former art teacher, Ms. Fleagle, have always encouraged me to accomplish more than I believed I could at the time. Such teachers are genuine and support students both in school and outside of the classroom. Ms. Fleagle, for example, had our outstanding artwork placed in the Piedmont Arts Museum in Martinsville, VA, after the items were removed from display at our public high school. The art portrayed people, specifically individuals with vitiligo, in their natural bodies and was deemed inappropriate by some people. These teachers also provided students with information about colleges, universities, and career opportunities available after high school. Ms. Fleagle suggested that I attend an art school after high school because it was a great opportunity to engage in what I deeply enjoyed. She helped me by sharing her thoughts on schools where I applied, and she motivated me to pursue my dreams. Though I did not attend an art school, I am pursuing my college degree, with a major in psychology with a special education minor.

While in high school, I also met teachers who had negative influences on students. These instructors, surprisingly, did not make me revert to being an unmotivated student. However, they did change my outlook on teaching and what should occur in the classroom. As previously stated, teachers who lack desired qualities are important. This is especially true for students who seek examples of "bad" teachers. Ironically, these teachers help students gain independence and model the characteristics students should not adopt if they decide to become teachers. In contrast to teachers who bring positive influences, other teachers are often disconnected from students. Most of these teachers "are not clear about their expectations, not fully present for their students, lack relationships with families and partnerships with community stakeholders, are not culturally responsive inside of the classroom and beyond, and do not provide opportunities for students beyond the classroom setting" (Ellis, 2021 p. 5). These teachers, like my former math teacher, did not set goals or boundaries for their students. Instead, they solely focus on academic work and fail to build teacher–student relationships in and outside of the classroom. Students who have similar teachers must learn to adapt and gain information from outside sources.

During my senior year of high school, I took a dual credit pre-calculus class. The teacher, Mrs. Wagoner, seemed to be an exceptional instructor with great reviews and an exciting personality. Although the teacher was great, there were many restrictions on how much in-person interaction we could have because of the COVID-19 pandemic. As a result of these limitations, students struggled in her class and often asked for help. Adequate support was not provided for those who requested assistance. Instead, nearly half of the students withdrew from the class because the teacher taught concepts too quickly, did not provide sufficient help, and failed to check for understanding.

Throughout high school, I witnessed many students crumble under pressure and stress because teachers did not change their methods of teaching. In many cases, these teachers seemed stubborn or confident in their abilities to listen to students. Their refusal to adjust instructional delivery during the pandemic negatively impacted many students. Another example is my former English teacher, who appeared to be preoccupied with her personal life. Although I occasionally enjoyed her class, this teacher graded assignments harshly and provided very little support. When students asked for assistance, she maintained it was not difficult and that we should not need guidance. Nevertheless, this teacher still made a positive impact on students regardless of how intolerant she appeared to be. Her students usually made great grades on their SOLs, and many of us have been successful with assignments in college.

As I entered college, at Radford University in Virginia, I became very invested in helping others. My interest in art remained, but I wanted to get a degree that would enable me to work with individuals who struggle to advocate for themselves. I also wanted to help those who struggle to learn and communicate efficiently. Many of these interests began to erupt after my youngest brother was diagnosed with an autism spectrum disorder (ASD). An autism spectrum disorder impairs social behavior and communication, and it appears differently for everyone who is diagnosed. I was introduced to my present major, psychology, in high school by a very influential teacher, Mrs. Mary Ann Graham. Mrs. Graham influenced my postsecondary decisions and remains in contact with me. She promoted diversity and openness in her classroom and treated all her students equally. Upon finishing this class, I decided that I would follow in Mrs. Graham's footsteps by pursuing a career that would allow me to support others. I decided to major in psychology and minor in special education.

During my second semester of college, after successfully completing a few general education classes, I decided to enroll in a special education course to broaden my knowledge and learn more about the major. I registered for a course taught by Dr. Antonio Ellis. It was nothing like I expected. The professor was extremely influential and impactful and proved to be one of the "warm demanders" described by Delpit (2012, p. 61). Dr. Ellis allowed students to flourish and learn independently, and he supported everyone in the class equally. He expected his students to do well, and he provided us with many great opportunities to improve our résumés and prepare for our futures.

Dr. Ellis had challenges that he had to overcome, yet despite those challenges, he taught effectively and efficiently. On the first day of class, he disclosed that had a speech impediment. Most of our classes were held online, but this did not stop Dr. Ellis and his teaching assistant from positively impacting students. I had never experienced having a teacher with an impairment or disability before, so taking this course was extremely beneficial and informative. Overall, this professor was one of the most understanding, comical, and genuine professors I have had. I learned a lot from him, and I believe that people with disabilities and impairments should be inspired by individuals like him. Despite being discouraged from entering the teaching field, Dr. Ellis went on to become an excellent professor who has achieved many accomplishments.

Overall, I believe that influential teachers are great assets and that they can potentially save students from failure. Regardless of how a teacher looks, acts, or speaks, I believe a teacher can profoundly influence students. This is especially true if teachers care for their students in a kind and appropriate manner, interact with students beyond the classroom, remain considerate of the individualized needs of each student, and provide students with tools that enhance independence and self-sufficiency. Broughton (2019) observes that "children do not care how much you know, until they know how much you care" (p. 34). Several of my teachers cared solely about academic work and their personal lives, rather than the well-being of students. As a result, their students were often confused in class and disapproved of the teacher's methods of teaching. In these instances, students sought external academic support to gain a better understanding of the information provided. Teachers who fail to provide reasonable support for students should strive, instead, to motivate students and inspire their determination to achieve success.

PRACTICAL RECOMMENDATIONS FOR ASPIRING TEACHERS

- As Gay (2018) stated, "Teachers who genuinely care about students generate higher levels of all kinds of success than those who do not" (p. 47). To that end, it is critical for teachers to show they care about students by providing them with opportunities to succeed academically and personally. Caring for all students requires dismissing stereotypes and biases.
- Student achievement in all grade levels is considered an important educational objective and outcome. Studies have measured student achievement in different ways through addressing school, family, and community connections, including the teacher's performance, students' language skills, and academic performance, attitudes, and healthy development (Sengul et al., 2019). Student achievement can be influenced on the individual level, the school level, the teacher level, or the parent level. I contend that it is important for teachers to be consistent, to be empathetic, and to develop healthy relationships with their students, their families, and the community.

REFERENCES

Broughton, A. (2019). *Evidence-based approaches to becoming a culturally responsive educator: Emerging research and opportunities.* IGI Global, Information Science Reference.

Darling-Hammond, L. (2006). Constructing 21st-century teacher education. *Journal of Teacher Education, 57*(3), 300–314.

Delpit, L. D. (2012). *"Multiplication is for White people": Raising expectations for other people's children.* The New Press.

Ellis, A. L. (2021). Mr. Linard H. McCloud: Clarifying excellence in teacher education practice. In A.L. Ellis, N. Bryan, Y. Sealey-Ruiz, I. Toldson, & C. Emdin (Eds.), *The impact of classroom practices: Teacher educators' reflections on culturally relevant teachers* (pp. 1–6). Information Age Publishing.

Gay, G. (2018). *Culturally responsive teaching: Theory, research, and practice.* Teachers College Press.

Sengul, O., Zhang, X., & Leroux, A. J. (2019). A multi-level analysis of students' teacher and family relationships on academic achievement in schools. *International Journal of Educational Methodology, 5*(1), 117–133.

CHAPTER 4

EDUCATORS PROMOTING GROWTH BEYOND STANDARDIZED TEST SCORES

Kaylee Golder

The older students get, the more likely they are to view school as an obstacle to their success (Gatto, 2012). They are often asked to follow a strict curriculum and standardized lessons, rather than to think about what life is like beyond the classroom walls. Yet this educational approach often holds students back from growing to their full potential as they try to fit to a rigid standard. As both a student and a teacher, I have seen this pattern multiple times. In fact, one of my own high school teachers treated her students as test scores and numbers, and she still torments my mind to this day. Fortunately, however, I also had a few exceptional educators who defied this status quo and had a long-lasting impact on my learning.

To begin, let me clarify my description of the extreme version of a classroom-limited teacher. My ninth-grade earth sciences teacher epitomized this approach. She was one of my first impressions of teachers in high school. I am a student who prides myself on my good work and grades. However, this teacher focused on standardized tests and how students performed based on the curriculum's standards. We were required to follow a strict no-technology policy and were not allowed laptops, phones, smartwatches, or anything not pertaining to the instruction. Her lectures and videos were as boring as the classroom environment, with the result that most of us simply "zoned out" during her class. For homework, we had readings straight from the textbook and study guides so tedious that if we didn't reference the page the information came from, we would lose points on the individual question. To receive a perfect score, it once took me 2 hours on the one study guide alone. Yet it was not my perfectionism causing this issue of needing a perfect grade; rather, the quizzes and tests were so difficult that every point was needed to pass the class. The tests were long and difficult, and eventually, most of my peers did not care about their class performance; they would rather give up than try and fail to meet her unrealistic expectations.

For most students, including myself, this class had to be taken in the first semester of high school. Consequently, I had an ongoing fear that high school was destined to be painstakingly hard and filled with teachers who had no concern for their students other than numbers and statistics. I was one of the few students in that class who kept going and received the letter grade I wanted, but for most of my peers, this one class alone ruined their grade point average (GPA). Not even the highest of scholars, the students with A's, got much from this course. This teacher was the one everyone knew by name and understood why her class was not worth the struggle. If I recall anything from the semester, it probably involves the secret group chats and code names we made up for this teacher.

In contrast, the first teacher who created a meaningful educational experience for me was my second-grade teacher. She was an upbeat teacher who focused on her students' well-being, yet still managed to teach. The class environment she created was the part that stood out for me. She was a teacher not bounded by the walls we were given, but only by the limits we students set for ourselves. I hardly remember the material from her class, but I remember two other important things: First, she was my favorite teacher up until seventh grade, and second, she always had her shoes off in class! While this may seem like an odd memory to stick in one's mind, it is the story I recall the most. She had a butterfly tattoo, and whenever she wore flip-flops, she took them off at various times throughout the day. Something as small as her taking off her shoes helped create a calm and relaxed environment, which made the space conducive for learning. I always found it fun and rewarding to show up to the class.

This inspiring teacher still teaches her second-grade class, and I can attest, from contact with one of her more recent students, that she still keeps her classroom fun and enjoyable. She does not worry if her students are following curriculum standards exactly; rather, she is more focused on what the students take away for the years to come. She does not limit her class to the standardized instruction, thereby allowing her students to learn and grow as the people they are. She knows her students well and encourages them to go further, and for that reason alone, she is by far one of the most notable teachers in her school.

Next, I cherished my seventh-grade algebra teacher. She remained my favorite teacher for a very long time. She not only had fun with her students, but she helped me grow as a full human being. Her teaching philosophy was not necessarily defined, but it consisted of multiple styles, trial and error, and a willingness to keep going. Her teaching style was everything; some days it would be textbook portions, videos, lectures and teachings, or something in between. This approach made classes, especially math classes, much easier, since the material you could not understand one day was explained differently the next. Another method she used was trial and error. When her lessons were not at a high standard, she accepted feedback and kept striving to be a better teacher for her students. I admired her for her giving heart and her perseverance. She was a new teacher at our school that year, but she kept going. Her class was not geared simply to following the instructions, but rather, to encouraging us to take the material and do something greater with it. She gave teaching her all, and I was always excited to see her. Some days I did not want to learn, but I was always willing to learn and grow in her classroom.

The teacher who taught my first-year English and my junior and senior-year creative writing courses rounds out my list of favorite teachers. As noted by the three different classes I took with this teacher, I was eager to sign up with him. His first-year English class was standard, with the bonus of personability and student input. But where his teaching methods truly excelled were in his creative writing courses. His belief was geared towards not limiting us as writers. More than half of the course material was student input, and any assignment could be modified if discussed before starting. Though he had guidelines and policies, he was willing to adapt and work with his students. He did not limit us to strict grammar rules, narrow writing choices, or papers alone. Instead, he always pushed us, from the first day of class until the day we graduated. At the start of the class, I felt I was a decent writer, with a computer, a notebook, and a pencil. By the end of my time with this teacher, I came out with those same materials, but also with a published magazine article, being listed as an editor for a published book, measurably better creative writing skills, and an eager and growing mind.

EAGER AND POSITIVE TEACHING

There was one distinct reason why my science teacher was the most dreaded teacher in my high school for me and many other students. In contrast, there are many reasons why my years with my favorite teachers remain as positive experiences in my mind. The first reason is because a teacher who comes ready, and even eager, to teach any student is a better teacher. Teachers who come to school ready and excited to teach, like my second-grade teacher, find themselves with students responding to them with the same eagerness and attention to learning. Students radiate off each other's energy, and they are more willing to learn from a teacher they like than from one they do not like. The difference between my worst and best teacher comes down to this: If a student is not only happy but also welcome to be there.

In short, teachers should avoid developing preconceived, limiting notions of their students and what a student can and cannot do. Students need an environment where they know their teachers want to see them succeed. Students who believe they are predetermined to fail are more likely to give up at the end of day and accept that failure is the only option.

This all-too-common student attitude has been described by researchers as "learned helplessness" (Firmin et al., 2004). For example, a number of my peers decided that because they failed the first few science tests, they were also destined to fail the upcoming exams. Unfortunately, largely due to their teacher's unhelpful attitude, this belief became a self-fulfilling prophecy for many of them. Conversely, good educators are teachers who stay optimistic, believe that their students can learn, and determine that no student is a "lost cause" at any point.

MULTIPLE TEACHING STYLES

Another trait of a positive, not negative, teaching is the use of multiple learning approaches. In my opinion, a teacher who believes all students learn the same way lacks fundamental knowledge regarding the science of teaching and learning from a neurological standpoint. Teachers must follow certain curricula, yet that does not mean students should be left out of the conversation. It is important that teachers not dictate the classroom; rather, the course and teacher alike should be centered on students' needs and progress (Bianco, 2002). Based on my personal experience, teachers who use several teaching methods to guide the students, from worksheets to hands-on activities, are more likely to engage all members of the classroom. Teachers who possess the ability to adapt the teaching methods based on their students' needs are extremely valuable.

COURSE TAKEAWAYS

The third belief I hold for teachers is making sure the students take something away from the course. Classrooms are places where students learn, yet learning should go far beyond the classroom. For example, I have found that classes that teach statistics and mathematical facts seem to result only in students retaining information for tests. Teachers of such classes come across not as inspiring educators, but merely as test preparation machines. In contrast, social science classes that teach life skills, history, and how people themselves create statistics are far more likely to develop well-rounded students. My science classes rarely provided information that we students could or wanted to relate to; however, in my creative writing class, I learned an enormous amount about who I was and what possibilities were available for me (Hollis, 2016). Based on my K–12 schooling experiences, I found that teachers who believe classrooms are the only location where learning takes place, only teach to the curriculum; they offer nothing beyond the classroom walls to support students in real-life situations.

CONNECTIONS

The last and most important quality a teacher must possess is the ability to build connections and relationships with their students. Teachers who build on the idea of social emotional learning—essentially understanding the person within the student—lead their pupils to much higher and improved success (Jackson et al., 2021). Teachers who see their students solely as learners, rather than as growing young people, lack the ability to see what students really need. The three teachers I rate as my best teachers were deeply connected and invested in their students as whole people. My class with the science teacher, who failed to connect with his students in any way, was by far my most challenging and unfulfilling learning experience.

CONCLUSION

The three teachers I learned the most from had positive attitudes, multiple approaches to teaching, and willingness to teach more than just the course material; most importantly, they cared about the whole student. Brown (2004) found that students do not respect teachers who assert themselves as authoritative figures while lacking empathy, and furthermore, situations where students lack respect for their teachers can result in many struggles for power (Brown, 2004). Instead, pupils choose to learn from teachers who possess an ethic of care. Teachers can choose to limit their experiences with students to teaching a mundane curriculum, or they can seek to build relationships with their students that extend beyond robotic teaching and standardized test scores. As a future teacher, I hope to deliver my curricula in ways that make real-life connections with students.

REFERENCES

Bianco, A. (2002). *One-minute discipline: Classroom management strategies that work.* Jossey-Bass.

Brown, D. F. (2004). Urban teachers' professed classroom management strategies. *Urban Education, 39(3),* 284.

Firmin, M., Hwang, C.-E., Copella, M., & Clark, S. (2004). Learned helplessness: The effect of failure on test-taking. *Education, 124*(4), 688+. https://link.gale.com/apps/doc/A121765622/OVIC?u=viva_radford&sid=bookmark-OVIC&xid=74f10cc8

Gatto, J. T. (2012). Life lessons are more important than school lessons. In J. Bartos (Ed.), *At issue: Do students have too much homework?* Greenhaven Press. (Reprinted from *Yes! Magazine,* 2009, September 9) https://link.gale.com/apps/doc/EJ3010796213/OVIC?u=viva_radford&sid=bookmark-OVIC&xid=15f9034b

Hollis, T. (2016). Wings and roots: Perspectives on resilience and academic success in education. In G. Wiggan (Ed.), *Dreaming of a place called home: Local and international perspectives on teacher education and school diversity* (pp. 101–119). Sense.

Jackson, K. C., Porte, S. C., Easton, J. Q., Blanchard, A., & Kiguel, S. (2021). Linking social-emotional learning to long-term success: Student survey responses show effects in high school and beyond. *Education Next, 21*(1), 65+. https://link.gale.com/apps/doc/A645314686/OVIC?u=viva_radford&sid=bookmark-OVIC&xid=ebdfd987

CHAPTER 5

DR. STIRLING BARFIELD

An Instant Role Model

Madison F. Keaton

Going to school is tough. No matter the age of a person, the location of the school, the classes taken, the school attended, or the grade level enrolled, school is difficult. As we all know, there are different factors for every person that impact just how difficult school really is. What is hard and/or stressful for one student may be easy or exciting for another student. Those who attend school in a city may or may not have more trouble at school than if they attended a school in a rural area. Infinite factors can make school an undesirable place to be. In fact, a recent study showed that approximately 75% of all students did not have a positive attitude towards school (Brooks, 2021). As with any problem, there is no single, simple solution. However, school problems can be much easier to manage and overcome with the assistance and guidance of a caring teacher. During elementary, middle, and high school, students are around their teachers more than their own families at times. Children of these ages are also very impressionable. Not only are they taught curriculum, but they are also indirectly taught by their surroundings, including their teachers. It is not unreasonable to say that teachers play a major part in raising many of our nation's children. In an article from 2019, career teacher Stacy Tornio writes that "the average teacher affects over 3,000 students during [his or her] career" (Tornio, 2019). This number shows just how important it is that teachers strive to be a positive light in students' lives.

From a personal standpoint, I am fortunate to have had so many caring and helpful teachers throughout my life that I struggle to count them all. I am appreciative of every single one. I never want to leave any of my teachers out of my personal "best" list, because they all deserve recognition. That being said, the teacher who has helped me most in my life is Dr. Stirling Barfield, also known as Dr. B. I would like to thank her for her contribution to my life thus far.

EMBRACING MY NEW LIFE AT RADFORD UNIVERSITY

I was about to graduate from New River Community College near my home in Dublin, a small town in southwestern Virginia, when I finally decided which 4-year university I wanted to attend. Almost everyone else from my high school class who wanted to attend college went straight into a 4-year university right after high school. To my knowledge, they all lived on their respective campuses and were doing great "adult" things with their lives. But I have always been very nervous about leaving my family, so I chose to enroll in community college first and transfer to a 4-year university later.

Finally I made the decision: I would transfer to Radford University, also in southwest Virginia, and commute an hour to school every morning and an hour back home every evening just so I could still be with my family. Truth be told, I did not want to attend a four-year university because my anxiety level was debilitating.

When it came time for Radford University's orientation program, called Quest, I was dreading it. I chose a 2-day Quest, and I could feel myself having a panic attack when they separated me from my mom. I did not know it at the time, but shortly after I had to leave my mother, I would meet someone who could automatically calm my fears. As I went with my group to the College of Humanities and Behavioral Sciences building, our group leader gave us all a little booklet and told us to pick a class to be a part of. Since I am a psychology major, choosing the psychology class was a no-brainer for me. When I walked in, I was greeted by an upbeat and positive professor. After we took our seats, she announced that her name was Dr. Barfield. Her positive energy and vibes were so contagious. Her energy was not overwhelming to me in the slightest. Instead, it instantly made me feel less stressed and welcomed. After she told us a little about herself, she gave us all a blue stress ball in the shape of a human brain. She made me laugh when she was handing them out, because she was upset that she did not bring enough for the whole class. She made a promise to students who did not get a stress ball. Consistent with her character, she kept her promise and made sure we all had a "blue stress brain." She also made sure to learn all our names in that short class period, and when she got someone's name wrong, she kept working until she finally remembered it. This automatically made me feel cared for and seen as an individual instead of just another new student coming to Radford. I saw so many people that weekend, and, as far as I know, Dr. B. was the only one who remembered my name. Everyone was very nice, but Dr. B. went the extra step. Later that day, she was assigned to help me with my schedule. Even though she had many students to help, she never once made me feel rushed in her office, and she treated me like I was the only student she helped the entire weekend. I was nervous about creating my first-ever schedule for a 4-year university, but it was a breeze because of her. Perhaps the most exciting part about my schedule was the fact that I was able to sign up for a class with Dr. B. It was only a one-credit class, but I was just happy to be in her class. She was my comfort zone. She was the professor for my class on orientation to the psychology major, and just like at Quest, she learned everyone's name almost immediately. She also told us that she saw several familiar faces from Quest, which made me even happier, because she remembered me even though it had been a month since I saw her last. In addition to our names, she let us share different things about our lives with the rest of the class, and she remembered these things as well. I had her class only on Monday afternoons, but she would always ask how our weekend was, and she would genuinely talk to us about it before class started. I could tell that she truly cared for every one of her students and their well-being. She even sent the class caring emails. The one I will never forget was when she dressed her dog up for Halloween and emailed us a picture. I loved getting an email about something like that, rather than always receiving emails about more work that I had to do. Throughout the semester, Dr. B. incorporated examples from stories we had told her about ourselves into her class lectures. She made the class personal to us, because she wanted to ensure we all got the help and knowledge that we needed. Due to her obvious interest in her students, her class was much more helpful to me than other classes have been; she addressed exactly what I needed in order to be successful.

We also had many class discussions. Normally I hate class discussions because I am so shy. However, I participated a lot in these discussions, because Dr. B. never once made me feel dumb about anything I had to say. My colleagues were supportive and nice to each other, and I firmly believe it was because of the way she handled our class.

Perhaps one of my favorite characteristics of Dr. B. was that she was transparent about herself to her students. Dr. B clearly had a rough life growing up, and she still became someone great. She never seemed like she was telling us to get pity; instead, she was telling us in order to motivate and inspire us. She wanted us to know that we could do as well, no matter how difficult our circumstances. She oftentimes told us about her financial struggles throughout college. Given this, she told us that if there were any of us that could not afford the textbook that was required for the class, she would find a way to help us out. I do not know if anyone took her up on that offer or not, but that meant the world to me for her to make such an offer.

She also catered to many different learning styles, which was helpful. As I neared the end of the semester, I was sad because I knew that I was going to miss seeing her. During exam week, I went to her office to visit. I was not planning on staying and talking to her. In fact, I was just going to give her a Christmas gift and leave, but she invited me in. I know she was busy, but once again, she made me feel as if I was the only student she had ever had, because she was so fully tuned in to what I was telling her.

MY NEW SEMESTER

Even though I am no longer in a class taught by Dr. B., I still see her quite often in the hallways of Hemphill Hall. There has never been a time when she walked by me and has not at least waved. There have been times that I have not even recognized that she walked by me because I will be looking down while reading my textbook, and she will get my attention and greet me. She also still remembers small details about my life that I told her at the beginning of last semester, and she follows up with me about those things. I have never felt more cared for as a student. Dr. B. always has a contagious smile on her face and is always friendly. Most importantly, she always cares.

Although she holds a doctorate, she is never boastful about it; she has faith in each one of us that we can obtain our doctorate one day as well—if we wish to do so. She never judges or treats anyone better than someone else. I believe that this is the main reason why so many students love and respect her. As Tornio (2019) writes, "75% of students say that teachers are mentors and role models" (p. 51). However, I know this number would be way higher if all teachers were like Dr. B. I am so blessed to have had her as a professor during my first year at a four-year university.

RECOMMENDATIONS FOR OTHER PROFESSORS

Although everyone is different, and we all have our own ideas about what qualities an inspiring teacher and/or professor has, the items listed here are the major reasons why Dr. Barfield inspired me. I believe that all of these are good attributes for a teacher or professor to have in order to make the biggest positive impact on students.

- Immediately try to get to know your students on a personal level. For many students, you may be the only person who seems to care about them.
- Learn their names if possible. This makes each student feel seen and respected.
- Keep in mind that a lot of students are struggling. Those who may seem the hardest to love are probably the ones that need it the most.
- Always welcome your students with a kind smile. You never know what they are going through.
- Incorporate your classes' specific needs into the lecture material. For some classes this is much tougher than others. However, making sure each students' needs are met is a necessity.
- Do not treat students as if they are beneath you.
- Be patient.
- Be understanding.
- Be a no-judgment zone.
- Provide various learning styles. No two students learn the same.

REFERENCES

Brooks, A. C. (2021, August 27). The real reason kids don't like school. *The Atlantic.* https://www.theatlantic.com/family/archive/2021/08/how-help-kids-like-school-better-loneliness/619881/

Tornio, S. (2019). *Twelve powerful statistics that prove why teachers matter.* We Are Teachers. https://www.weareteachers.com/teacher-impact-statistics/

CHAPTER 6

MRS. LEONA K. BROWN

What an Extraordinary Teacher Looks Like

Allison G. Brown

A great primary teacher is essential for all students. The first teacher someone has sets the tone for the rest of one's school career and possibly one's entire life. Primary teachers can make or break a student's success. In my case, I was fortunate enough to have the most wonderful teacher as my first. Mrs. Leona K. Brown was my Pre-K teacher at Hillsville Elementary School. Mrs. Brown was and still is the best teacher I've ever had. She had the biggest impact on me by far out of the hundreds of teachers and professors I've had.

Jackson (2021) and other researchers have confirmed that good teachers possess a number of specific, essential qualities and characteristics that make them effective in the classroom (Ellis et al., 2021). In my view, Mrs. Brown possessed all the characteristics of a great teacher. One of her greatest gifts was empathy. She always made every student feel loved and cared for, and she always made me feel priceless. She never raised her voice, and she never showed frustration. She remained patient and treated everyone with respect.

Mrs. Brown was a great teacher for many reasons. She employed classroom strategies that are often utilized by skilled teachers. One of her strongest skill sets was her unwavering ability to manage the classroom. She had the perfect balance of positive and negative reinforcement. She gave positive feedback to students throughout each day. She was always specific when telling students exactly what they did right, and that approach encouraged other students to do the same. She encouraged and praised progress.

Her main goal, above any positive reinforcement, was building positive relationships with students. Many great teachers build strong relationships with their students and their students' families. Broughton (2021) points out how important it is for teachers to build positive relationships with their students and their students' families (Ellis et al., 2021), just as Mrs. Brown did. She learned what every student liked and didn't like and kept those things in mind when doing activities in class. She recognized that she could make an enormous difference in her students' lives. She found out what her students' strengths and interests were, and she emphasized them. In employing these techniques, she created opportunities for success. (NICHCY, 2011).

One thing I will always remember from her class is the thinking tree. She created a tree of construction paper on her wall and put a chair beneath it. If a student was making bad choices, she would have that child sit at the thinking tree and raise a hand when ready to talk about his or her actions. Sometimes she would sing a calm-down song with the student, then explain that it was time to do problem-solving. She then asked the students to tell her what they did wrong, how they could fix it, and what they would do differently next time. Lastly, they were able to rejoin the class. If students weren't ready when they raised their hands, Ms. Brown would go back to her regular activities until they were.

Another strategy she used when students weren't doing what they were supposed to was, "If you don't want to do it now, you can stay in from recess and practice." Usually, students complied after the threat of losing recess time. If they did not, they would have to practice for a duration of recess. I love both strategies, because they allow students to know they are in control of their own outcomes. They chose whether they got to participate as part of the class or not. Many students learned from these strategies and made decisions that led to their desired outcomes.

Mrs. Brown also was great in communicating expectations. In her class, I always knew what I did right or wrong, and I learned from it. I plan to use this type of behavior management in my own classroom.

Mrs. Brown also collaborated with other teachers to raise the likelihood of success for students. She met with her aides and grade-level teachers frequently to plan as a team. She met with kindergarten teachers to capture the skills her current students needed to prepare for kindergarten. Thereafter, she worked diligently to ensure students learned those skills.

Collaboration was also a great feature in her classroom. I worked at tables in groups often and rotated in centers with different classmates. She changed one center a few times throughout the year. At one point it was a kitchen, then a vet center, and then an office with appointment books. I had so much fun in the centers, as they were always filled with exploration and adventure. In the mornings we focused on the calendar and weather. She used songs and patterns to help students better understand the rotation of calendar dates and weather changes. We also had little cars that moved places for classroom helpers. Mrs. Brown also did lots of music, dance, and movement. We had frequent brain breaks and sometimes played games for learning. My favorite dance we did was the Tooty Ta. I know I will do this fun dance with my future students.

If there is only one thing in Mrs. Brown's classroom I could remember, it would be the mountain of books. She had books from A–Z. She believed reading was the key to success and always encouraged us to read. She read to us multiple times a day and used different voices to make the characters come to life. Young stresses the importance of teachers making time for books in and out of their classrooms (Young et al., 2008). Teachers should make time to read aloud to their students and let them read for enjoyment on their own.

One thing I aim to have, like Mrs. Brown, is an abundance of creativity. This energetic teacher always had so many activities and ideas! My classmates and I were always engaged, because she used so many different hands-on activities that we were interested in. She made school enjoyable, which motivated me to learn. I developed a love for learning in her class, and I am sure this foundation is one of the reasons I performed well in school ever since.

Sometimes Mrs. Brown had us do activities just for fun, like putting shaving cream all over our tables, carving pumpkins, making spider crafts, and making pumpkin patch pudding. She even put spider webs with spider rings all over the classroom. Parents or grandparents often came into the classroom and participated in these activities with us. We had Grandparents Day, "spooky ghost feet" day, where parents painted ghosts on our feet, and a potluck lunch where we made and wore turkey hats. Even if a student did not have a parent or grandparent come, Mrs. Brown made sure that someone came into the classroom to make that student feel special. We also had field trips to a pumpkin patch, a movie theater, a dinner musical theater, and lots of parks and playgrounds for picnics. On our special "farm day," we built dirt babies who grew grass as hair. As the grass grew, we gave them haircuts. Another creative activity Mrs. Brown arranged was class parades around the school. For example, we had a costume parade and a teddy bear parade.

I loved all of these events, but my favorite part of Pre-K was the parties. We had a Christmas party where we each received our own stocking, a Valentine's Day party with a little post office for our Valentine cards, a fall festival with hayrides and inflatables, a nursery rhyme tea party where we dressed up with our parents, and an Easter party with an Easter egg hunt on the playground. One time we built our own little gingerbread houses and made gingerbread cookies in class. Then, Mrs. Brown made a huge gingerbread house we could all go inside. One night during the Christmas season, Mrs. Brown hosted a Polar Express night, where all her students and families came to the school in pajamas. She read the Polar Express book to us, and we did arts and crafts. Another night we had a Cat in the Hat party, where a real Cat in the Hat came and visited us. The week prior was Dr. Seuss week. We read all the Dr. Seuss books and even helped make green eggs and ham in class. On Cat in the Hat night, we had a birthday cake for Dr. Seuss. My favorite of all these memories was when a leprechaun came to our class on St. Patrick's Day. We never saw him, but there were tiny green footprints all over our classroom, even in the fish tank!

According to Lewis (2021), one of the reasons he wanted classes with a certain teacher was because that teacher was known to be a fun teacher (Ellis, 2021). No matter what the grade level, letting your students have fun is so important. Children—and college students and adults as well—love to have fun while learning. I do not have many memories of elementary school, but I remember almost everything from Pre-K like it was yesterday. Even though it was 15 years ago, Mrs. Brown made that year so much fun, so memorable and special, that I will never forget it.

Mrs. Brown was also expert at adapting to her students' needs. She met all her students where they were academically, building upon their areas of strengths and strengthening their areas of need. I, for one, struggled early in school. I had a speech impairment through most of elementary school, and I had difficulty reading on grade level. I was in the special education program working with a speech pathologist to meet my individualized education plan (IEP) goals. At the time, I did not know that I was any different from the rest of my classmates. In hindsight, the reason I did not realize I was behind was because of Mrs. Brown.

Jackson (2021) encourages teachers to accept students unconditionally regardless of their differences, noting that children should feel that they are more than their problems (Ellis et al., 2021). Mrs. Brown never made me feel less than the other students, and she didn't single me out or make me feel different. I always felt like I belonged. This acceptance set the tone for me for all the years I was in special education. I never viewed it as a weakness. I only viewed it as another part of my school day. I tested out of special education in three years and have not struggled with speech or reading since. I owe a lot of this success to Mrs. Brown. I had other wonderful teachers to help me along the way, but I know my journey would have been much different had I not had Mrs. Brown as the first teacher to ignite progress and set the tone.

Mrs. Brown was and still is truly the best and most inspiring teacher I have ever had—although I must confess that something does make my favorite teacher unique: Mrs. Brown is my mother. Even though it may seem like she is my favorite simply because she is my mom, I know this is untrue. I am positive that even if she was not my mom, and I only knew her as my Pre-K teacher, she would still have been the best teacher I've ever had. In the school setting alone, she made the strongest impact on my life. It was unlikely that my mom would be my teacher, but it was truly a blessing for me academically that she was. She really is the best teacher I could have ever had.

Many other people who worked with Mrs. Brown, had her as a teacher, or knew her as a teacher said she was by far the best teacher they had ever met. She is such an inspiration for me and for others. Having her as my teacher inspired me not only to do well in school but to strive to be a good person in general. She single handedly inspired me to go into education. I remember pretending to be teaching like Mrs. Brown, my mother, when I was four years old. Growing up and watching her, I have been reassured that the field of education is where I am meant to be. She inspires me to be an exceptional teacher. I have dozens of ideas for my own classroom stemming from my Pre-K experience alone. My dream is to go into education and be just like her. Many people tell me they strive to be half as good as my mom in the classroom, and I know I will strive to carry on her legacy in my own classroom when the time comes.

Mrs. Brown is now a principal and is furthering her impact on an entire school instead of just one classroom. The position she holds as my favorite and most inspiring teacher remains untouched. I was behind in elementary school for multiple reasons, but I graduated from high school with GPA above 4.0. I have excelled academically, possess a very creative mindset, and have loads of inspiration for my own classroom. I give a lot of credit to Mrs. Brown for my achievements so far. Without such an amazing primary teacher, I would have lagged so much more behind in so many areas. But instead, I had a wonderful first school-year experience.

To conclude: In my view, having a great introduction to school is essential. My Pre-K setting pushed me to be outgoing and to have fun. I was able to be a child in Mrs. Brown's classroom. I have confidence that I can do great things for my students, because Mrs. Brown modeled greatness for me. She always pushed me to do and be my very best, and I can never thank her enough.

RECOMMENDATIONS FOR CURRENT AND FUTURE TEACHERS

- Build relationships with your students.
- Don't forget to let them have fun.
- Have great classroom management techniques.
- Be creative.
- Be patient.
- Read all the time.
- Remember primary teachers set the bar for all teachers who follow.
- Strive to be like a teacher you loved or were inspired by.

REFERENCES

Broughton, A. (2021). Turning up with the torch: The transformational power of a legacy of male "warm demanders." In A. L. Ellis, N. Bryan, Y. Sealey-Ruiz, I. A. Toldson, & C. Emdin. (Eds.), *The impact of classroom practices: Teacher educators' reflections on culturally relevant teachers* (pp. 7–18). Information Age Publishing.

Ellis, A. L., Bryan, N., Sealey-Ruiz, Y., Toldson, A., & Emdin, C. (2021). *The impact of classroom practices: Teacher educators' reflections on culturally relevant teachers.* Information Age Publishing.

Jackson, J. T. (2021). Trying a different approach: The influential power of Mrs. Taylor and Mr. Johnson in seeing an ugly duck turn into a swan. In A. L. Ellis, N. Bryan, Y. Sealey-Ruiz, I. A. Toldson, & C. Emdin. (Eds.), *The impact of classroom practices: Teacher educators' reflections on culturally relevant teachers* (pp. 65–76). Information Age Publishing.

Lewis, J. (2021). High expectations: The key ingredient of academic success. In A. L. Ellis, N. Bryan, Y. Sealey-Ruiz, I. A. Toldson, & C. Emdin. (Eds.), *The impact of classroom practices: Teacher educators' reflections on culturally relevant teachers* (pp. 77–84). Information Age Publishing.

National Dissemination Center for Children with Disabilities. (2011). *Speech and language impairments.*

Young, T. A., Bryan, G., Jacobs, J. S., & Tunnell, M. O. (2008). *Children's literature, briefly.* (7th ed.). Pearson Merrill Prentice Hall.

CHAPTER 7

HOW A FIRST GRADE TEACHER CHANGED MY LIFE

Joleigh Helton

I first knew I wanted to be a teacher in kindergarten, at 5 years old. From the very moment I stepped foot into the classroom that I was going to call my second home for the next school year; I knew I wanted to be in an environment like that forever. My love for school and teaching has overcome all other obstacles that have been presented within and out of school. The impact my teachers had on my life has been unforgettable throughout my schooling experiences and life's journey. I have been inspired by my teachers—both the influential and the inferior—in every stage in my life.

Throughout elementary school, I had many influential teachers. They all were knowledgeable and effective within their teaching styles, and they allowed for sincere relationships to be formed with every student. However, my first-grade teacher has been my most influential role model in my educational journey. She made the most significant difference in how I view the profession and all the joy you can experience while teaching. In my opinion, she possessed all the necessary skills needed, and more, to be the perfect teacher.

Given that the teaching profession is among the top five list of "most prestigious occupations," it takes very knowledgeable individuals to accomplish every intricate task needed (Torino, 2019). My first-grade teacher's passion, beauty, ability to build relationships, listening skills, fun-loving nature, preparedness, and caring personality inspired me.

First of all, she was passionate about her job. Every day as we came into the classroom, she appeared delighted to see us and to have the opportunity to teach us. As a student at the time, this feeling was indescribable. She made me feel as if I was a gift to her and that I had a greater purpose, much more than just sitting in her classroom and learning the material being taught. She was similar to a mother to all thirty of her students; she appeared to love us like we were her own children. Anytime we needed support, additional help, or just someone to talk to, she was prepared to help us at any cost. I cannot recall a single time when she was angry or frustrated with any student. She showed such a passion for teaching! Along with that passion came all the other characteristics she needed to be an effective teacher. She made me want to stay in first grade forever.

To me, my first-grade teacher possessed an external and internal beauty. She had a beautiful heart and soul that aided in her success as a teacher. However, she never noticed how influential and beautiful she truly was. Rather, she made it her mission to make sure her students knew how beautiful, remarkable, and unique they were. When we walked into the classroom each morning, she welcomed us by saying how appreciative she was that we came to school and were a part of her class. (Since then, I have never had another teacher who vocalized how glad she was to have students spend the day with her.) Throughout each day, this extraordinary first-grade teacher commented on our inward and outward beauty. She made it known what she loved about each student. For me, it was my kind heart and ability to stay positive, which has stuck with me for over 15 years. She also made it known how important we were in the lives of our parents, caregivers, and families. Furthermore, she wanted all her students to feel significant in all aspects of their health, safety, and personality. At 6 years old, my foundation for loving life and school was established.

My teacher built relationships with us as her students. By the end of the first week of school, she knew all of our names, favorite colors, birthdays, and what we wanted to be when we grew up, in addition to whom we lived with. Each of the pieces of information allowed her to connect with us on a deeper level, more than if she had learned personal details about us throughout the year. My teacher also understood that each student learned differently, which required different modifications and accommodations. She capitalized on her understanding of the individual needs by making her lessons multifaceted, while still being able to manage the whole class.

This skill takes preparation. I hope that one day, I too will have the skills to balance my classroom and build relationships like my first-grade teacher.

My first-grade teacher was a patient listener. She would always talk to us about anything; including what we did last night, how we felt, what we were going to do after school, how our siblings were, and anything else that peaked her interest. Her inquisitiveness also supported our classroom being transformed into a community, which made the academic year enjoyable (Barile, 2020). Even in the later years, when we were no longer her students, she would stop us in the hallway to inquire about our well-being. As someone considered to be a teacher's pet, I talked to my teacher every moment I got. I did not realize it then, but I am so appreciative that she listened to everything I had to say. It felt like she was listening for hours to my imaginative 6-year-old mind.

My first-grade teacher was also a storyteller. Not only was she an exceptional listener, but she could tell and read us stories unlike anyone else. Every morning after the entire class arrived, we discussed what we did after we left school the day before. She always began the discussion with what she did, as I sat in amazement regarding the out-of-school activities. I always asked her questions about what she did, and she would repeat the story in greater detail. I believe her stories expanded my vocabulary. After lunch every day, it would be story time, when she read *The Magic Treehouse* or *Junie B. Jones* books aloud to us. She usually read two or three chapters a day. When she read, she made me feel as if I was a character in the story. This was my favorite part of school because she made it so engaging.

My first-grade teacher was filled with joy. In a 6-year old's mind, school is a place where lessons are taught in order to prepare for adolescence. Although learning is the premier goal, it does not have to be boring. Because of my teacher's enthusiasm, I was very excited to come to school to find out what we were going to do each day. I especially looked forward to Friday dance parties, as we danced to the song titled *Celebration* by Kool & the Gang. This almost 5-minute-long song allowed the entire class time to move, dance, be social, and have fun at the start of every Friday morning. In addition to motivating my entire class, my first-grade teacher also gave herself something to look forward to each week that aligned with her teaching styles and the class's enjoyment (Bell, 2018). She danced with us for the entirety of the song, and then moved on with our academic lessons for the day. Observers may have viewed our dancing as abnormal; however, none of us cared because we were having the time of our lives celebrating, while also learning. This song demonstrated how we had made it to the end of the week and provided us an opportunity to celebrate our academic efforts. Upon waking up on Friday mornings, I always looked forward to the celebration moment.

My first-grade teacher was consistently prepared. When I was in her classroom, I truly thought she worked magic. She had the skills to move from one lesson to another without us knowing we were beginning something new. Each day flowed smoothly, which made school hours seem to go by quickly. However, we were never bored. She would teach full lessons and have activities prepared that were tactile pertaining to the material we just learned. She never had us waiting to begin an activity, unless it was a chatty day for the rest of my classmates. Even then, she moved right along with what we needed to complete before the buses arrived. Her expertise and knowledge allowed her to develop the skill of true preparedness.

My first-grade teacher exuded an ethic of care. Because she knew practically everything about her students, she knew what was important to us. So, in return, what mattered to us became important to her. One memory I have was close to the end of the school year when we were getting ready to go onto the playground. As the class was lined up, she asked if anyone needed to use the lavatory before we left. I raised my hand. I went to use the lavatory with a pair of sunglasses perched on the top of my head. Before washing my hands, I was fixing my hair and the sunglasses fell in the toilet. In panic mode, I quickly washed my hands and told my teacher that my sunglasses fell in the toilet. She knew they were my favorites, so she went into the bathroom and retrieved my sunglasses out of the toilet. This is just one example out of many that shows the level of care my teacher had for her students. This is still a memory I will never forget about my first-grade teacher, who was understanding about a situation out of her control. She aided me in every way she could, in the classroom and beyond (Gagnon, 2019). Most, if not all students in my class have similar stories about an instance where this thoughtful first-grade teacher showed how much she cared for them. Her passion and the things she cared for most were her students; this caring attitude was evident to us throughout our time in elementary school.

To be an effective teacher requires passion, intrinsic beauty, an ability to build relationships, listening skills, a joyful nature, preparedness, and an ethic of care. If not born with these attributes, an individual should desire to gain these traits in order to become an effective teacher. To be an effective teacher, passion and love must overflow within every task and lesson. Building relationships should be a primary goal of a teacher. A teacher must listen and be able to be listened to in order for respect and learning to occur. Joy should be intertwined in the fabric of the classroom setting. The teacher should be prepared to aid in classroom management and stressful situations. A caring nature is needed to manage a classroom, causing students to feel a sense of safety.

Being a teacher is difficult, even from a student's perspective. However, difficulty does not define the teacher, the student, or the classroom.

Teachers must strive to develop the skills to handle the varying experiences and needs that each young student brings.

RECOMMENDATIONS FOR CURRENT EDUCATORS

- Care for all students the same, no matter their differences.
- Before anything else, make relationships with every student.
- Respect is given, not earned. The same goes with communication and trust.
- Act like you are the student's only role model.
- Remember that words affect worth.
- Treat every activity as if it is your favorite.
- Display your enthusiasm, or the class will be dull.

REFERENCES

Barile, N. (2020). Ten things every new teacher should know. *Hey Teach!* Western Governors University. https://www.wgu.edu/heyteach/article/10-things-every-new-teacher-should-know1808.html

Bell, L. (2018, December 26). *How teachers can stay motivated during difficult times.* https://www.larry-bell.com/how-teachers-can-stay-motivated-during-difficult-times/

Gagnon, D. (2019). *10 qualities of a good teacher.* Southern New Hampshire University. https://www.snhu.edu/about-us/newsroom/education/qualities-of-a-good-teacher#:~:text=Some%20qualities%20of%20a%20good,a%20lifelong%20love%20of%20learning

Tornio, S. (2019). Twelve powerful statistics that prove why teachers matter. *We Are Teachers.* www.weareteachers.com/teacher-impact-statistics

CHAPTER 8

MS. HART AND MRS. GILBERT

The Inspirations of a Future Educator

Taylor Poff

As a future educator, I know that the teachers and professors I have had throughout my time in elementary, middle, and high school and college have had great impacts on me and my chosen career path. I distinctly recognize two phenomenal educators whom I consider the most influential teachers and professors I have crossed paths within my life. The first is my third-grade teacher, who first inspired me to pursue teaching. The second is my favorite college professor, whom I had during my sophomore year of college and who restored my love for the field when I began to think that maybe education was not the line of work for me.

    I cannot remember much from third grade, but I do remember it being the year that I first started thinking about pursuing a teaching career. My teacher, Ms. Hart, always brought so much life and energy to the classroom every morning. She had a great sense of humor that had the class laughing until our stomachs hurt. I remember her reading novels to us while we sat on the rug nearby, absorbing her storytelling skills. It seemed that Ms. Hart made a point to have a relationship with each of her students to the degree where she knew all of us and our differing personalities and interests well. I remember thinking to myself that, even though we were only third-graders, she treated us like adults. She never talked down to us and always expected our best effort, no matter the task. I remember coming home after school during this time and trying to teach my younger brother the same things Ms. Hart taught me. I watched her inspire students daily and then I would come home and try to do the same with my brother. My mother still brings out old pictures of me reading novels to my little brother at our bedtime when we were young, just as Ms. Hart did in my class.

After Ms. Hart inspired me at such a young age, I started dreaming of becoming a third-grade teacher. I stayed set on this idea until my senior year of high school, when the pressure of choosing a career path and a college loomed over me. I felt that teaching was too ordinary for me at this point in life. I wanted to try bigger and better things that would take me places where I had never been before and would allow me to have unique experiences. This change of plans left me feeling lots of anxiety and uncertainty about my future.

When it came time to choose a college and a major, I chose Radford University and English education, because at this point it felt safe and I truly did not know what else I could do. I was sure that I would be transferring schools and switching majors multiple times after making this decision, because I felt my heart was not in education anymore; it had just become monotonous and typical for me. I merely "went through the motions" my first year of college, remaining open to new possibilities that might lead me elsewhere. By sophomore year, I felt that I would remain as an education major, simply because I had no idea what else I would be interested in or good at. Little did I know that the spark for education I once had was soon to be reignited.

I remember the first day I walked into Dr. Gilbert's class. It was English 402: Teaching Writing. I walked in and sat down, feeling the usual nerves and anxiety that comes with all first days of class. I took a seat near the back of the room and got settled. As soon as Dr. Gilbert came in and placed her belongings, students could tell simply by her mannerisms that she was not like the average college professor. She did not wear the professional or prim and proper demeanor that many professors display. Somehow, even from that first day of class, Dr. Gilbert always seemed approachable and as an equal to the students. White (2009) contends that classrooms where "the teachers are approachable and encouraging" are most often well-organized, well-managed classrooms. Dr. Gilbert's classroom was an excellent example.

Dr. Gilbert made it clear that she was continuously learning new things in life just as we were. We started class with the normal icebreakers. Thereafter, she got conversations going among all of us, including herself, as part of introducing the course. I always preferred the reading aspect of my English courses rather than the parts of my classes that involved intensive writing, but I found myself looking forward to the rest of the semester with Dr. Gilbert, regardless of whether exhaustive writing was involved or not.

One of the most memorable classes I had with Dr. Gilbert occurred just prior to our project on narrative writing. She went through an exercise where she asked us to take a few minutes to pick two or three moments in our life that were some of the most memorable moments we could think of. She asked us to write each memory down and then sit and ponder them for a few minutes. After some time had passed, she asked us to narrow down our ideas and choose one memory we felt we could elaborate on the most. Once we had narrowed down our topics, she introduced a prewriting exercise. She explained that she was going to set a timer for 5 minutes, and during those 5 minutes we were to write as much as we could, as fast as we could, about our chosen topic. She said that it didn't matter what we wrote, as long as we were writing during the entirety of the 5 minutes.

Once the timer began, I remember scribbling down several thoughts until my hand became exhausted. I looked up to see how much time was remaining and saw Dr. Gilbert's eyes focused on her own notebook, while her hand scribbled away furiously. Dr. Gilbert was doing the exercise with us. After the timer went off, she prompted us to share what we came up with during our 5 minutes and how we thought the exercise helped us generate ideas for the prewriting stage of our narrative projects. She shared what she wrote during the exercise as well. This remained a constant theme in anything that Dr. Gilbert asked us to do: She actively participated in her own exercises and assignments to promote class engagement and discussion. I appreciated this aspect of her class. It truly displayed how much she cared about her role as an educator. As researchers have noted, this collaboration or partnership between student and teacher changes "the understandings and capacities of both sets of partners—making us all better teachers and learners" (Cook-Sather et al., 2014, p. 6).

I also appreciated how Dr. Gilbert graded our assignments. She primarily graded based on progress rather than performance. For instance, when we wrote papers for her class, she had us turn in everything we did in the writing process. This included our prewriting, our rough drafts, peer reviews from other classmates, final papers, and a self-reflection on our final drafts after we had finished the writing process. We were successful on the assignment if we completed all parts of the writing process and turned in the progress we made in writing the paper. Keeton (2016) refers to this method as grading through a portfolio, writing that "a portfolio or other similar collection tools can be beneficial for the teacher as well as the student. For the teacher, a portfolio can function as a record to judge a student's effort more accurately. It can also illuminate the kind of effort a student is making"

(p. 13). After the progress grade, Dr. Gilbert critiqued our final papers, giving us suggestions for revisions or clarity and commending us for what we did well. After we received the performance grades, she always gave us the chance to revise our final papers another time to better exemplify the constant revision in the writing process.

Dr. Gilbert's class prompted me to experience the same feelings I felt long ago in third grade when education first became my dream. She made education feel like an extraordinary field, one that matters much more than it seems to on the surface level. Based on my experience with the two favorite teachers I have described, I believe that if educators are genuine and approachable to their students, as opposed to displaying dominance and superiority, students will feel more comfortable participating and engaging in classroom activities. I also assert that working alongside students, participating in the assignments and exercises you assign, shows your humility and interest in what you are teaching. This teaching model causes students to be invested in and intrigued by your course and assignments. Lastly, not assessing students solely on their final outcome is very beneficial in a classroom. Students need to know that their hard work and efforts are acknowledged, regardless of their level of mastery.

REFERENCES

Cook-Sather, A., Bovill, C., & Felten, P. (2014). *Engaging students as partners in learning and teaching: A guide for faculty.* John Wiley & Sons.

Keeton, S. (2016). Effective and meaningful grading in applied collegiate voice: Assessing effort and progress, a grading toolbox, and a recommendation. *Journal of Singing, 72*(5), 563–71.

White, B. (2009). *Student perceptions of what makes good teaching* [Paper presentation]. Teacher Education Crossing Borders: Cultures, Contexts, Communities and Curriculum. The Annual Conference of the Australian Teacher Education Association (ATEA).

CHAPTER 9

THE IMPACT OF AN EDUCATOR

Brooke E. Kelly

As an aspiring educator, I often think about how I may impact the future generation of learners. Most people do not think of the teaching profession as making a deep impression on future generations; however, teachers are in everyone's lives almost every day from the age of four until young adulthood. Throughout these years, students encounter educators with different styles and personalities. Scholars of human growth and development contend that during these encounters, students are constantly growing and developing. Given their daily interactions with students, educators are uniquely positioned to make significant contributions to the intellectual and social emotional growth of young learners and indeed, to humanity at large. This impact can be positive—or it can be negative. Either way, students typically remember the impact each teacher has had on them.

In high school, I originally had the idea that I was going to attend college to major in nursing. Due to my career goal, I took an anatomy class, where the teacher impacted me in a great way. Mrs. Caldwell not only inspired me as a student, but also as a person. She was kind, positive, and always wanted to see her students be successful. Anatomy is not an easy course of study, and I definitely learned that the hard way. When documenting the positive impacts of a teacher, most students reflect on a course in which they experienced success; however, this is not the case for me. In fact, it was how Mrs. Caldwell handled my failures that made her stand out to me. She never singled me out for doing worse on a test than other students, and she always chose to build me up rather than tear me down after I earned a failing grade. When I finally earned a passing score on a test, Mrs. Caldwell was genuinely happy for me. Despite all my failures, she knew I aspired to become a nurse. Therefore, she always encouraged my dream.

Mrs. Caldwell not only cared about her students as learners, but also as individual people. Countless students stayed after class to talk to her about life and receive advice, myself included. Mrs. Caldwell always desired to see us succeed in every aspect of life. I believe that teachers such as Mrs. Caldwell, who care about students as both learners and unique human beings, make the greatest impact. By forming connections with students, teachers are better able to understand their learning styles and help them enjoy the art and science of learning. In the article titled "How (and Why) to Encourage Failure in the Classroom," teacher Maria I. Teixeira (2019) provides tips on how to be encouraging, like Mrs. Caldwell, as opposed to discouraging, like many other teachers, when working alongside students who are failing. Teixeira's observations about humor and playfulness have been particularly inspirational to me. "Incorporating some sensible humor into your class can never go wrong" (p. 5) she writes. "Being theatrical, playful, sarcastic (with care), and silly can sometimes lead students to realize that you are not an authoritarian figure, rather, a human being who is there to help" (Teixeira, 2019, p. 7). I think the most important part of this comment is that teachers can be seen as normal human beings. When teachers are viewed in this light, students will not be afraid to talk to them and share what they are experiencing.

Going back as far as elementary school, I never had another teacher who stood out in an exceptional way. However, one teacher did capture my attention. She was my fifth grade math teacher, and she was notorious for making students cry. I did not think anything of this as a young student, until I experienced her myself. I was sitting in the front of the class taking notes when all of a sudden, my teacher stopped and looked at me. She realized that my notes were not reflecting what she was teaching. At that point she stopped and scolded me in front of the entire class. She pulled up a chair and sat next to me and stared as I frantically copied notes from the chalkboard while everyone else sat silent. Not only was it embarrassing, but as a student I felt like I was slow at note taking compared to my peers. This traumatic memory is still embedded in my mind. Overall, my time with this teacher was an unfortunate experience modeling the characteristics I do not want to exhibit as a teacher. I have always told myself I will never have the reputation like this teacher did for making students cry.

As a result of these experiences, I learned valuable lessons from the view of a student and an aspiring teacher. Over the years, I have gotten better at test taking, and I also am a lot faster at taking notes than I was in fifth grade. However, I did not need a teacher to degrade me in front of the class for me to improve my note-taking skills. As a teacher, if a student is struggling in any aspect, my response will never be to tear them down but rather build them up, just like Mrs. Caldwell. I know that words of encouragement can go a long way.

Besides words of encouragement, finding resources to help students succeed can be very beneficial. Such resources be readily available to every student.

Listed below are some of the lessons I took away from the K–12 teachers I encountered:

1. When a student fails a test or assignment, a teacher's first response should never be anger and frustration. Teachers should respond by figuring out possible barriers and dismantling them. As teachers, you never know what your students may be going through in their personal lives. Therefore, it is important to make personal connections so you can employ individualized, student-centered strategies for them to learn, achieve success, and be free of fear in the classroom.
2. Educators should understand that students' mental and physical needs must be met before they are able to fully learn. These unmet needs can distract the student from learning. For example, if a student is going through a tough time mentally, whether it is from something happening at home or from a diagnosed disorder, this issue should always be addressed and assessed before they are expected to put efforts into learning. There are also basic needs such as food, water, and the proper amount of rest, all of which are necessary for students to give their full attention to learning. In the article "Focusing on Student Emotional Needs," du Preez (2021) discusses the importance of meeting these emotional and physical needs. An exercise described at the beginning of the article stood out to me. du Preez writes: "The social-emotional needs of students play a huge role in classroom culture, and they have never been more artfully illustrated than in the viral 'I wish my teacher knew...' social media exercise by third-grade teacher Kyle Schwarz. This exercise offered students the space to reveal struggles with homelessness, battles with self-esteem, and doubts about their future" (p. 14). The results of this simple exercise show that

teachers are often oblivious to what is going on behind the scenes in students' lives. There are countless students who are too afraid and ashamed to share details about their personal lives. Therefore, it is important to have safe spaces and resources readily available to support students beyond academics.
3. For me personally, kindness and enthusiasm go a long way as a teacher. I have encountered teachers who behaved as if they dreaded their career. Their constant nonchalant dispositions made me uncomfortable with attending their classes. In contrast, teachers who were outgoing, kind, understanding, and excited to be teaching were far more enjoyable to be around. As a K–12 student, I was more enticed to learn and engage in those teachers' classes. In turn, these teachers benefited because students wanted to listen and remained attentive, making it easier to deliver lessons in a tension-free environment. As Zhang (2014) points out in the article "Teaching with Enthusiasm: Engaging Students, Sparking Curiosity, and Jumpstarting Motivation," the importance of a teacher's attitude cannot be overstated. Zhang states,

> Although student behavioral, cognitive, and emotional engagement can be influenced by a myriad of contextual factors, including teachers, peers, family, community, and culture, the teacher variable assumes a crucial role in determining student engagement in the classroom. (p. 54)

4. Students often reflect the energy teachers give. Simply put, if the teacher is excited to be present in class, then most students will reflect that same excitement. If a teacher is eager to teach a new lesson, then the students will be eager to learn. Teachers should always model their expectations from students.

Having a variety of teachers, both the good and the bad, taught me valuable lessons as an aspiring teacher. My teachers showed me things I want to implement, and things I want to avoid, in my future classroom. I will mirror Mrs. Caldwell by always encouraging my students when they struggle academically. Nor I will not embarrass my students in front of their peers.

As part of the upcoming generation of teachers, I am optimistic and inspired by the hope that students with mental health or emotional disorders, disabilities, and other struggles will be treated equally in the classroom. Under the care of a caring teacher, these students will have the resources they need to ensure both their social emotional well-being and their academic success at school.

REFERENCES

du Preez, S. (2021, March 15). *Focusing on student emotional needs.* EVERFI. https://everfi.com/blog/k-12/focusing-on-student-emotional-needs

Teixeira, M. I. (2019). *How (and why) to encourage failure in your classroom.* Education First United States. Education First Teacher Zone Blog. https://www.ef.edu/blog/teacherzone/encourage-failure-classroom/

Zhang, Q. (2020, November 24). *Instructor's corner #3: Teaching with enthusiasm: Engaging students, sparking curiosity, and jumpstarting motivation.* National Communication Association. https://www.natcom.org/communication-currents/instructors-corner-3-teaching-enthusiasm-engaging-students-sparking-curiosity#:~:text=An%20enthusiastic%20teacher%20often%20spices,jumpstarts%20their%20motivation%20to%20learn

CHAPTER 10

A TEACHER OF LOVE, COMPASSION, AND AN INFLUENCE

Christian R. Worley

Teachers are taught to use a multitude of methods to target children's educational needs. One of the most effective ways to gain access to a child is "self-love, love of beauty, compassion, and a love for learning," writes Lory Hough, author of *What's Love Got to Do With It?* (Hough, 2022). Love is an unmeasurable foundational block in the continuance of younger generations' education.

Yet the topic of love is often perceived as a conflict when mentioned or associated with the field of education. "Very little has been written about how love impacts teaching and learning," Hough (2022, p. 96) writes. "Love and beauty cannot be evaluated in the traditional manner, so educators often shy away from them." In part, this reluctance may be due to an automatic assumption of inappropriateness. How can teachers show love within the constraints of the modern everyday classroom?

The best educators are assumed to be passionate about teaching; passion is a complex form of love and understanding for the field as well as the subject of study. "One can teach basic skills without love, but to truly make a difference in a student's life, there needs to be love," Hough (2022, p. 105) writes. "Love sees teaching as an art where we explore different ways of connecting to subject matter and to students. Love brings patience and understanding, which are so important in teaching" (Hough, 2022, p. 112).

These teachers make a mark on their students that can last a lifetime. Patience, compassion, and understanding are key ingredients in managing and operating a successful classroom. According to Hough (2022), "Compassion allows us to see our students as individuals who are struggling and sometimes suffering. It also allows us to see ourselves in the student, including the student who we find is hard to relate to" (p. 88). Love, compassion, and influence are the keys to the making of a well-rounded educator. Through her love, compassion, and influence, one individual educator in my high school years completely uprooted and rerouted my life goals, plans, and trajectory, helping me achieve my goals as an adult.

My transformation began my first year in high school. When walking into the main entrance of Union High School in the small town of Big Stone Gap, Virginia, on the first day of classes, I was greeted with a warm welcome from faculty and staff. Of course, in high school, you hear every rumor under the sun about every teacher and student. Hearing rumors of one teacher made me especially anxious, knowing that at some point I was guaranteed to be placed in her classroom. I had many classes with fantastic teachers while in high school; however, not one teacher or student prepared me for what was to occur.

It was the first day of my junior year when I received my schedule and realized that I had been placed in the advanced English classroom taught by the one teacher I dreaded having, Mrs. Blanken. I was terrified of what was to come in the following semester because of the monstrous rumors that I had heard about her as an educator. The first time I walked into the classroom, I was welcomed with a warm "Hi there, hello," and a pearly white smile. I was a little put off by the warm introduction; however, I instantly knew from the first time meeting her that the rumors could not possibly be true. She continued throughout the day showing how excited she was to make each individual student successful in her classroom. As the semester continued, we bonded over a passion for creative writing and the love of learning that we both desperately craved. We both enjoyed escaping into another dimension as we dove into a new book for the next class assignment or some form of captivating exercise. Mrs. Blanken had a true passion for both the English language and teaching the young minds placed before her.

Being passionate about what one is learning is a key ingredient in the success of the student as well as the educator. As Hough (2022) explains, "Love of learning means keeping the child's natural curiosity alive. This also allows space for students to pursue their own interests. Teachers often feel the need to cover the curriculum. Therefore, sometimes there is little opportunity for students to question and explore" (p. 97). Mrs. Blanken always had the students' interests and passion as the focus of her teaching methods and practicum. Not once did I ever feel the need to worry about the well-being of my education or any other students in the classroom.

As Mrs. Blanken continued to teach and allow the students to flourish and grow in their own direction, she strived to make the best out of every day. The semester continued with no slowdown in the sustained effort shown by Mrs. Blanken, as well as her students. We felt her concern and compassion every day. Nucaro (2018) writes, "Teachers should model compassion and acts of compassion on a daily basis, by complimenting students on their successes, inquiring about their day or their weekend activities, and addressing all bullying behaviors consistently" (p. 99). Mrs. Blanken embodied this compassion in ways that were meaningful to educator and the student alike.

As we learned in her class, Mrs. Blanken had gone through challenges that few people ever face in a lifetime. She had been gradually going deaf since she was a teenager, and while I had her as a teacher, she was having to read lips, because her hearing was eventually going to get to the point of no return. Even with this troubling condition, she continued to teach passionately and with ambition. As the semester came to a close, Mrs. Blanken recommended that I enroll in her creative writing course in the following spring. I, of course, agreed and proceeded to add the class to my schedule that very day. Though I could not have explained it at the time, I recognized that Mrs. Blanken embodied the characteristics Caplan (2022) describes as common to first-rate teachers:

> Perhaps it's the most obvious of characteristics, but a good teacher is dedicated to their work and educating their students. "Love" and "passion" are often tossed around when considering how much a teacher puts their heart into their work, but dedication takes the cake. A dedicated teacher not only has a passion for their job and loves to teach, but also consistently works to make their classroom a better place for all. (p. 98)

When we returned to school in January after our Christmas break, we could never imagine what would occur in the following months. While participating in the creative writing course, Mrs. Blanken was enthusiastic about using nature and our hometown as the basis of all assignments. I had never truly appreciated the hometown that I have until then. The class continued with a breeze, until tragedy struck our entire community.

On March 10, 2019, most of the community woke for church, when they were flooded with news that a local police officer had been in a car crash and that he had died. However, this was not the case. The officer, whom I knew to an extent, was the nephew of Mrs. Blanken. As the day progressed more information came to light. The incident was devastating: The authorities ruled it a domestic murder-suicide. Knowing this officer and the family he was raised in, I felt that this could not possibly be the truth; however, the decision was finalized. This occurrence devastated the entire community. Of course, one particular group was affected most: his family. Mrs. Blanken requested time off from work to focus on the well-being of her family and herself. She was (and is) brave, full of love, and dedicated to her family, students, and community.

The level of dedication that Mrs. Blanken displayed to her job, her students, her community, and her family is truly admirable. It was during this tragic time for her family and our community that I realized I wanted to follow in her footsteps. I wanted to be an influence on my future students as an educator, just like her.

How does one define an influence? "Influence can be defined as having an effect on the character, development, or behaviour of someone or something. Teachers influence students in many different areas of students' lives, not only academically but socially as well" (Cotnoir et al., 2014, p. 1). Mrs. Blanken is the definition of what I consider to be an influential teacher. She always strived to make an impact. As we approached the end of the semester, I was debating on running for office in the Student Government Association. Her influence led to my final decision and my election to the SGA during my senior year.

I began my senior year in the fall of 2019 knowing that I wanted to pursue a degree in music education. Again, Mrs. Blanken's influence led to my focus on a career in education. While everyone expected our senior year to be smooth and perfect, we did not imagine a global pandemic occurring in the midst of it all! Mrs. Blanken held Union High School together as we all felt as if the entire building would fall to the ground with the news of school being interrupted and moved online due to the COVID-19 pandemic. However, Mrs. Blanken's perspective was always positive; she knew this experience would make us stronger individuals.

A few years later, I sat in the lounge of a dorm at Radford University, studying for my Bachelor of Science with a double major in music and psychology, with the hopes of attending graduate school. My plan has obviously changed over time, from becoming a high school band director to having the dream to teach at a collegiate level in music theory and cognition. Though my career goals have evolved, I have never lost the dream of teaching. Education is a field with many options and opportunities, not only for the ones pursuing a career in the field, but also for the students. For me, experiencing the long-term impact a successful teacher can have has been mind boggling.

Educators are never the same and should never be compared to one another; however, in my view all teachers should strive for the level of love, compassion, and influence demonstrated by Mrs. Blanken.

REFERENCES

Caplan, Z. (2022). *Every great teacher has these 7 qualities in common.* https://fairygodboss.com/career-topics/becoming-a-teacher

Cotnoir, C., Paton, S., Peters, L., Pretorius, C., & Smale, L. (2014, July 24). *The lasting impact of influential teachers.* https://files.eric.ed.gov/fulltext/ED545623.pdf

Hough, L. (2022). *What's love got to do with it?* Harvard Graduate School of Education. https://www.gse.harvard.edu/news/ed/18/08/what%E2%80%99s-love-got-do-it

Nucaro, A. (2018). *The value of compassion in teaching.* Edutopia. https://www.edutopia.org/article/value-compassion-teaching

CHAPTER 11

WHAT IS A QUALITY TEACHER?

Looking Beyond the Intellectual

Maddison Parrish

For years the question, "What qualities make a good teacher?" has been asked by both educational researchers and practitioners. Are academic qualities all that matter, or does good teaching go beyond that? "There's a big difference between being a teacher and being a good teacher" (Western Governors University, 2020, p. 6). Being a good teacher involves qualities that go beyond just academics. Being knowledgeable about your subject is important, but your relationship with your students goes farther than knowledge in a classroom. Teachers need to be personable. They need to be able to relate to students and show they care about them by practicing empathy and patience (Western Governors University, 2020). Based on my personal experience, I believe that students who feel understood and supported by their teachers are much more likely to be successful in the classroom

In this chapter, I use a traumatic schooling experience I encountered to respond to the question of what makes a quality teacher from my perspective. I conclude the chapter by offering recommendations to teachers.

I first considered this question in-depth during my high school junior year AP calculus class. Before my junior year at Salem High School, I was excelling in school. I was the kind of student most of my peers wanted to model. When I started high school, my grade point average (GPA) remained at a 4.0. My GPA led to my winning academic awards. I had the best grades among all my friends and was known as a teacher's favorite. Because of my work ethic, I almost never struggled academically and rarely needed outside help.

Prior to my junior year, I never faced an academic challenge in school. Looking back, I redirect most of my challenges in that class back to the teacher. I think Mr. M. lacked the characteristics needed to be considered a good teacher. Thinking about Mr. M. brings me back to the notion that being a good teacher goes beyond the ability to convey academic content. Without a doubt, Mr. M. was extremely intelligent. He graduated at the top of his class at the U.S. Military Academy at West Point and earned degrees in engineering. He most likely could teach calculus half asleep. The question is, if Mr. M was so knowledgeable, why did his students struggle so much in accessing the content he taught?

The second day of my junior year I decided to enroll in the advanced calculus course. I knew it was going to be a very challenging class; however, as I mentioned, I had always performed very well in school. Therefore, I anticipated doing well in calculus. Nonetheless, I was not prepared for the challenge I faced in Mr. M's class. On top of the extremely challenging curriculum for the class, I had a teacher who seemed not to care about teaching. His attitude made the course seem impossible to pass, which also contributed to my struggle to learn the content. Before this experience, I never realized how much a teacher 's attitude could negatively affect a student's academic success. In reflecting, I think part of the reason I always achieved academically in school was due to supportive teachers who had specific student-centered qualities. Therefore, when I encountered Mr. M., who lacked all these qualities, it was a very different experience.

The first few weeks of the class were fine. However, I was beginning to recognize the challenges I was experiencing. During these few weeks I had very little interaction with Mr. M. The only interaction I had with him was when I informed him about transferring into the class. Without welcoming me at all, he simply said "find a seat." Mr. M. had no idea who I was since I was not listed on his roster, and he did not ask for my name or any other identifying information. After our initial encounter, I got a sense that Mr. M. was not an approachable person, so I distanced myself, waiting for him to embrace me as a student. Based on my observation, he did not seem to have a relationship with any of his students. There were a few highly gifted students he occasionally interacted with in the hallway, yet he appeared to avoid extensive conversations with students.

As the semester progressed, the lack of communication worsened. I noticed we did less math every day. At the beginning of the year, we spent the entire class doing math. Thereafter, we began spending around 85% of the class periods doing math. Eventually the time spent doing math dropped to around 50% of class period and lower. By the middle of the year, we would do only one math problem a week. Students enrolled in this class were not learning from their teacher at all. Instead of learning calculus, we spent the class period playing games on the smartboard. Once a week we would take maybe a 5-minute break from playing games to do a single math problem. It became very clear to us that Mr. M. did not want to be there; therefore, his attitude transferred to the students. He seemed not to care if we learned anything in the course or not. I dreaded the class every day and always tried to find excuses not to attend. This reaction was very unlike me, because historically I always found pleasure in attending school. My disposition was a sign something was wrong, particularly when I tried to find every excuse possible to avoid attending this class.

Mr. M. did not hold his students to any standards. Since we were not learning calculus during class sessions, most of us performed poorly on assignments. Mr. M. indicated that our performance on assignments was our responsibility and that he was not empathetic. As students, we tried to voice our concerns by telling him how we felt, but he would just tell us we were not working hard enough and received the grades we deserved. To put this situation into perspective, the majority of the class received grades averaging around 20% on tests. This confused me, because I could not understand how a teacher could not show concern when most students were performing extremely low.

The primary issue I had with Mr. M. was his refusal to help students. Since we were not doing any calculus in class, I fell behind on learning new content. I constantly asked for help and his response would simply be "No!" Because I desired to learn calculus, I would ask him if I could stay late or come in early for extra help, yet to no avail. This refusal of help took a toll on me because I did not understand why he was not willing to help. Teaching and providing academic guidance for students were his responsibilities, and he blatantly refused to do either. As previously mentioned, prior to enrolling in this course, I maintained a 4.0 GPA and never asked for help. Therefore, building the courage to ask Mr. M. for help took a lot from me and was discouraging. It became clear that he did not care about me as a person, let alone my performance as a student of calculus. Midway through the school year, I gave up because I did not know what else to do.

Having such a negative experience in this class impacted me in several ways. My performance in this course caused tension between my parents and me. I received an F in calculus on progress reports. My parents were upset due to my low performance. They did not understand how an honor roll student with a 4.0 GPA average suddenly failed a class with extremely low grades. I tried to explain that we played games every day in class instead of doing work, and that I asked Mr. M. for extra assistance, including asking to meet outside of class time. However, my parents did not believe me. They could not believe that a teacher would conduct himself in such a way, so they just assumed I was not being truthful. They concluded I was not trying and therefore I blamed Mr. M. for my failing grade. This took a huge toll on my relationship with my parents, because we were constantly fighting about my performance in calculus. I was at a loss because I felt powerless and without agency. It was a very stressful school year, which had a very negative impact on me mentally, psychologically, and physically. This traumatic experience also chipped away at my self-esteem. I was not accustomed to struggling academically. I earned an F majority of the year, completing the course with a D average. This lowered my grade point average tremendously. I maintain that it was unjust that all the hard work I invested for my soaring GPA was diminished because of a teacher's unwillingness to teach.

However, I think one of the biggest impacts this negative experience had on me was from a future teacher standpoint. I always remind myself that Mr. M. is the perfect example of what I do not want to become as a teacher. I want to be the opposite of him. As a student taking the calculus course, I thought the course delivery lacked integrity. Nevertheless, in hindsight I learned what not to do as a teacher. I never want to duplicate those bad practices in my classroom. As I am going through my curriculum as an education major, I often think back to Mr. M.'s class to remind myself of what type of teacher I want to become.

RECOMMENDATIONS FOR TEACHERS

My recommendations for becoming a good teacher reflect my own experiences as a student, as well as insights from some of the educator-researchers I have studied in my college courses. To summarize:

- Show students that success can mean many different things.
- You will get a lot more from your students if they know you care about them.
- Be present, interact with students, and be supportive.
- Create a welcoming environment and make accommodations accordingly to ensure each student has an equal opportunity (Friend, 2018, p. 26).
- Maintain a balance between support and independence.
- Build a teacher-student relationship with each student.
- Show an ethic of care.

REFERENCES

Friend, M. (2018). *Special education: Contemporary perspectives for school professionals* (5th ed.). Pearson.

Western Governors University. (2020, October 19). *Top qualities and skills of a good teacher.* Western Governors University. https://www.wgu.edu/blog/top-qualities-skills-good-teacher2001.html#close

CHAPTER 12

INSPIRED BY AN AFRICAN AMERICAN MALE ENGLISH TEACHER

Jabin Walker

From elementary to high school, I had pretty good teachers. However, a few individuals stood out to me and have impacted my life. These teachers are a part of the reason I am where I am today. I grew up in a small town in South Central Virginia called South Hill. My mother was a college graduate, and my father was a correctional officer. They always taught my sister and me that college is the way to go, especially for people of color. I held to this and lived by it for the most part, and I wanted to attend North Carolina Agricultural and Mechanical University. In 2012, I started middle school at Park View Middle School in my hometown. It was here that I realized that I wanted to attend college after high school. The people I associated with had higher education ambitions, which motivated me to do well by earning good grades. It was not until my eighth-grade year that things came together, when I met an English teacher named Mr. Hargrove. Although I had a great father who was loving and caring and a provider for his family, Mr. Hargrove became my role model outside of my family.

Lift Every Voice, pages 65–66
Copyright © 2024 by Information Age Publishing
www.infoagepub.com
All rights of reproduction in any form reserved.

I remember seeing him for the first time and thinking to myself, "Who is this Black man with such poise and confidence in himself?" I had never seen a Black male teacher before, and I adamantly wanted to be like him. Mr. Hargrove was a member of Kappa Alpha Psi Fraternity Incorporated, a Black Greek letter organization founded at Indiana University in 1911. Some of the things he learned from being a member of Kappa Alpha Psi carried over into his way of teaching. For example, he started a boy's group called Men of Valor. I did not know that many things he introduced to us were adopted from Black Greek life. These early influences later inspired me also to join a Divine Nine Organization.

Fast forward to high school. I started to take a different path, one that did not involve seeking higher education but working instead. I began to take classes like building trades and auto mechanics until my 12th-grade year. In the first semester of my senior year, I met the second teacher who changed my life. Mr. Watkins was extremely helpful to me. He challenged me and pushed me to be the best student I could be and helped me decide which college I should attend.

Mr. Watkins made his class fun and exciting, while challenging his students. It was not long before I remembered Mr. Hargrove and my college dreams, which motivated me to start applying to colleges. I applied to Radford University under its early acceptance admissions. Once accepted into the university, I told Mr. Watkins the good news and informed him that I was thinking about going to Virginia State University (VSU). What he told me next was the sole reason why I am at Radford University today. He recommended that I enroll at Radford as opposed to Virginia State. Mr. Watkins told me that he had graduated from VSU, and that he thought Radford would be an overall better experience for me. A year later, in the fall of 2019, I arrived on the campus of Radford University. I soon joined Alpha Phi Alpha Fraternity, Incorporated, which I consider to be the greatest fraternity on earth.

Overall, I am very thankful for everyone who was involved in helping me get to where I am in life, including my mother and father, Mr. Hargrove, and Mr. Watkins. These two Black male teachers changed my life for the better and helped me realize the importance of higher education.

CHAPTER 13

OVERCOMING THE HARDSHIPS OF MY EARLY EDUCATION

Katherine L. Wagoner

As I reflect on my K–12 educational experiences, I find that I remember more teachers who made a negative impact on my life rather than a positive impact. However, these teachers allowed me to reflect and form ideas about the kind of teacher I would like to become. I thank them for modeling what not to do as a teacher. Throughout this paper, I will describe situations that impacted my learning and thoughts about becoming a teacher.

Throughout elementary school, I was a child who was always full of energy. I loved socializing with my classmates. Unfortunately, my first-grade teacher was not a fan of mine. She frequently wrote notes to my mom saying I was a problem in her classroom. She would single me out every day in class in front of the other students. She even went as far as moving my desk out in the hallway one day because she was "tired of hearing my voice." As a young child between the ages of six and seven, I did not comprehend why I was being separated from my peers. Considering how my teacher treated me, I interpreted her actions as meaning that I was always doing something wrong. Meanwhile, my behaviors were appropriate for children in my age group at that time. Every morning, I would cry to my mom not to go back to school because of the way this teacher made me feel. One situation I remember especially clearly was when, after recess one day, I asked to go to the restroom, and she refused to let me go. She explained that I should have gone during recess instead of running around on the playground. She then let other students use the restroom before she let me. I ended up having an accident, and she made a point to humiliate me in front of the whole class. She handed me a trash bag and I was to sit in it until my parents came and got me. I eventually transferred to another school because my parents saw the negative impact the teacher was having on me.

The next teacher I remember is my second-grade teacher. This teacher made a positive impact on my life. I feel that she was the first teacher who understood me. She believed in me. I remember looking forward to attending her class every day. Her classroom was warm and comforting. She had a soft-spoken tone and never raised her voice at students. Unlike the previous teacher, she was a teacher who showed that she cared about the wellbeing of students. Every day we had a different activity that was hands-on and interactive. Given that I am a kinesthetic learner, I excelled in her class. I particularly enjoyed the small reading groups. My fondest memory was when we read *The Little House on the Prairie* (Wilder, 2007). The teacher wore clothes from the time period and brought artifacts to help us gain a better understanding of the content. I admired her teaching methodology and relatability to students. She inspired me to want to become a teacher, using her teaching style as an exemplar to model. Even when I became a high school student, I still made time to visit my second-grade teacher. She always expressed how proud she was of me and affirmed my dream of becoming a teacher.

This is the kind of teacher I strive to be. She is an example of how healthy K–12 teacher–student relationships can have a lifelong impact on the student's trajectory. Just like my teacher, I want to have a positive impact on my students when I become a teacher. This type of impact has less to do with academics and more to do with human connectivity.

The final teacher I remember is my fourth-grade social studies teacher. In contrast to my second-grade teacher, my experiences in her fourth-grade class were negative. She was an outstanding teacher academically. She also engaged in hands-on learning and engaging activities with students. Unfortunately, she prohibited me from participating in most class activities. As opposed to allowing me to intermingle with my peers, she made me complete worksheets at a secluded desk away from everyone else. I did not understand why. As a young child, this constant separation and seclusion was detrimental to my self-esteem. At the beginning, the teacher separated me from my peers within the classroom setting. As time went on, she removed me from the classroom altogether to complete worksheets. I typically would be told to complete my assignments in the in-school suspension room. I recall this classroom being extremely small, tucked away in the basement with a wooden squeaky door. I remember sitting in that room crying, because I did not understand what I had done wrong. My teacher never provided an explanation for why she segregated me from my peers. This teacher inflicted emotional trauma on me. I learned to associate socialization with punishment.

The following school year, I was diagnosed with chronic anxiety—at the age of 12. In addition, due to my traumatic experiences with teachers, I also became more reserved in school. I did not talk as much in classes or participate in class discussions unless I was forced to do so.

I share my K–12 schooling experiences to highlight how children's experiences with teachers can have a lifelong impact. It is important for teachers to remember that children are naturally impressionable. Therefore, it is incumbent upon teachers to serve as role models who motivate students to be their best selves. In hindsight, I thank my fourth-grade teacher for modeling the type of teacher I should not become.

While I remember other experiences in K–12 schools, these are the three encounters I learned the most from as I consider my future career as a teacher. I contend that one challenge of being a teacher is balancing your status as an authority figure with the willingness to have an ethic of care for students. The most important takeaway from my reflection is that teachers' relationships with students are critical. A student's level of comfort with a teacher can have implications on mental health and academic performance. Every child deserves a teacher who ascends beyond academics and cares for their well-being from a wholistic perspective.

REFERENCE

Wilder, L. I. (2007). *Little house on the prairie.* HarperCollins.

CHAPTER 14

A TEACHER'S ENCOURAGEMENT LED ME TO COLLEGE

Jada Turner

I have always been known as an energetic, happy, and engaging student. I am often the student who breaks the silence and volunteers first to respond in class. With these tendencies and impulses, I have also become the student who is reprimanded for my participation and eagerness. To my peers, I am often perceived as the "pick me" girl, the girl looking to be the center of attention, or the one who needs instant gratification and reassurance from others. I continue putting my best foot forward, participating when I feel like I have something of value to add. After years of judgment, I realized in my third year of college that I had begun to dial down for others. I stopped myself from participating because I was terrified of what others, especially my professors, would think.

I was born in North Carolina and given the opportunity to attend a year-round STEM (science, technology, engineering, and mathematics) elementary school. While attending this school, my entire outlook on education changed. As a kindergartener and first grader, I was often in trouble due to excessive talking and disruptive behavior, which resulted from boredom. During my matriculation in a school that did not have a curriculum or resources to challenge me as a learner, I found myself struggling to maintain friendships and good behavior, and I experienced a steady decline in my academic performance. While continuing my education in North Carolina, I came to a crossroads after learning my family was relocating.

When my mother moved to Virginia, she unknowingly left me in an abusive environment. My fourth-grade year was extremely difficult. I became totally responsible for taking care of my two younger siblings. I went from being a well-performing student to being absent, tired, irritable, and depressed, causing my grades to plummet. I started not liking school due to the dysfunction I was experiencing at home. Instead of asking for help, I lashed out at my teachers. During this time, I felt a sense of hopelessness.

The next year, I reunited with my mother. During this time, I enrolled in Virginia Public Schools as a fifth-grade student. I still had a disdain towards education and became an average student who did just enough to be promoted to the next grade.

Throughout this transition, I needed layers of academic support and wraparound services in order to achieve success. I still desired to foster connections with my peers and teachers, even though I dreaded the school environment.

I remember several unique experiences once I started middle school. I recall being given three popsicle sticks in my eighth-grade science class. Each time I raised my hand, asked a question, or gave an answer, I had to turn in one popsicle stick. The purpose of this class participation strategy was to limit the number of times students verbally participated in class. Eventually, I lost all interest in participating, causing me to lose my title of being a gifted student. My experiences both at school and home had a detrimental impact on my mental health and academic performance.

When I started high school, I discovered my love for music and structure, as I was beginning to work through my trauma and mental instability. I had a teacher who took an interest in my well-being and overall success. During this time, I joined my school's ROTC program and was offered an opportunity to have paid opera lessons through the Norfolk Academy of Music. I started challenging myself in my required classes and began to enjoy my life as a student again. My teacher did not reprimand me or label me as annoying. I was celebrated for my strengths and supported through my weaknesses. Finally, I felt accepted and embraced in a school setting. My teacher consistently provided leadership opportunities for me and encouraged me to enroll in advanced placement (AP) courses.

The summer before my senior year of high school, I started thinking about life as a high school graduate. After considerable self-reflection about my future, I decided to enlist in the military. I was convinced that I was not college material. A part of me felt that I was not smart enough to succeed at a college or university. As a back-up plan, I thought that joining the military created a pathway to success for adults. Thereafter, I watched friends of mine who graduated start the process of moving on college campuses.

Seeing my friends excited about starting college made me rethink my choice to join the military. During my high school years, I had become friends with some of my teachers. Those were the individuals I turned to when I became distraught over my post high school plans. As I grappled with my decision, I decided to subtly mention the idea of attending college. My teachers quickly affirmed my decision and continued encouraging me to at least consider college as a viable option.

Since I had endured so much instability as a child, I often felt compelled to find validation in my choices. Once I received my teachers' blessings, I continuously thought about college enrollment. I started applying to schools every time I had the opportunity, and I researched what life might be like for me as a college student. I felt it was important that I make an informed decision. One day the school I attended hosted a Radford University onsite admissions event. After applying and being accepted, a year later I found myself registering at freshman orientation

Since my first day of classes as a first-year college student, I have continued to persevere, regardless of mounting challenges. During my freshman year, I noticed my inability to focus. My inability to focus made it extremely difficult to be successful as a college student. My junior year at Radford brought about new challenges, as I was diagnosed with attention-deficit hyperactivity disorder (ADHD). With this new discovery, I asked myself, "How has no one noticed?" This diagnosis was never mentioned or considered during my earlier years of schooling. Typically, children are diagnosed with ADHD in elementary and middle school, although some are not diagnosed until high school. The more I thought about why no one noticed, the more I was reminded of my hyperactive behaviors in elementary and middle school.

I realized that this diagnosis explained my behaviors. Instead of seeing my diagnosis as an inability, I found a deeper meaning in my diagnosis. Knowing that I had ADHD gave me the courage to confront situations, ask questions, and ensure that I received the accommodation needed for me to achieve success. I learned that there is value in controlling my impulsivity, including listening to others. My ADHD diagnosis allowed me to explore my needs and be successful without a strenuous amount of effort. Prior to my diagnosis, I had calendars, reminders, and sticky notes, which created disorganization in my brain. I created coping mechanisms and exhaustive strategies that worked for me. Now that I better understand my condition and receive treatment, I am better positioned to achieve success academically.

As I reflect on why no one noticed my ADHD as a young child, I consider the environment where I was raised. I always felt like I needed to be the happy or smiling child. Concurrently, I always felt like a burden on everyone in my environment. Being repeatedly told that I was an issue as a child made me overly self-conscious. Instead of being a child who asked for support, I believed in being self-sufficient. I decided to be resilient by taking charge of my personal and educational needs. Instead of being invisible, I became an excellent student with great behavior and outstanding grades. With all my efforts, I still was not recognized at home for my accomplishments and tenacious determination. At school I craved the attention I did not receive within my household. Regardless of my efforts not being acknowledged, I still felt the need to always be perfect, so I went the extra mile to further enhance my performance. I desired to be praised as a student.

Now, as an advanced college student, my purpose for participating in class has changed. In my formative years, I participated for gratification and approval. However, I now participate because I have valuable opinions and am genuinely passionate about the content being taught.

I encourage teachers to avoid having bias or preconceived notions regarding any student. In addition, I strongly believe teachers should work hard to ensure that all students are included, valued, and supported within the educational milieu.

CHAPTER 15

THE EFFECT A GOOD TEACHER HAS ON STUDENTS

Jenna Staton

As I have chosen to pursue a career in the field of education, reflecting on my own experiences in public school has helped me to acknowledge how certain teachers have positively impacted my life, inspiring me to be proud of who I am today. While many teachers have had a wonderful impact on my life, my English teacher in my senior year of high school has inspired me in a multitude of ways on different occasions. Mrs. Andrea Johnson taught me many life lessons that I will carry with me for the rest of my life and into my career. I thank Mrs. Johnson for her wonderful impact on my life, as she has shaped me to be the woman that I am today and who I want to be as a future educator.

THE IMPORTANCE OF EXPRESSING PRIDE IN STUDENTS

In Mrs. Johnson's class, she made sure that all her students felt welcomed and that her classroom could be considered a safe place. During my time in her class, I never felt judged when I came to her with a question or when I needed help. When I chose to confide in her with private information, she communicated her thoughts in a non-judgmental manner. I remember a moment when I realized that Mrs. Johnson showed pride in her students in many different ways for using their voices. In this meeting, we reviewed a paper I had written, and she provided feedback on it. With this paper, students were instructed to write about an obstacle they had faced in their life and how they overcame it. My teacher encouraged us to dig deep with this topic, instructing us to think of something that we truly felt had impacted our lives. With this assignment, I chose to step outside of my comfort zone and write about my battle with an eating disorder. As a shy student, I was nervous about the reaction of my teacher once she read the paper. However, my teacher's reaction was the complete opposite of what I expected. While reading the paper, my teacher was not judgmental about my education. Instead, she expressed her pride in my ability to rise above this battle and become stronger from it. Her comments were optimistic, and she was thrilled that I was strong enough to write about this battle. She also told me I had achieved resiliency at a young age and that I needed to use my struggles with an eating disorder to help others.

Mrs. Johnson's words of pride and kindness touched my heart. These words are a reminder to me in any situation that I am stronger than the battles I face. As this example shows, educators should recognize that pride is an important emotion to express to students on all levels. Whether in the K–12 grades or college, expressing pride in a student has been found to have positive benefits. For instance, studies have found that pride can help to increase the self-esteem and productivity of a student (Nielson & Lorber, 2009, as cited in Etherington, 2019). Because pride has been proven to have such positive impacts on students, it is important for teachers to find ways to express pride in their students whenever the opportunity arises.

THE POSITIVE IMPACTS OF HEARING AND RESPECTING A STUDENT'S BELIEFS

With my English teacher, it was obvious that showing respect and acceptance towards all her students' ideas, beliefs, and simply who they were as individuals was a priority to her. Students of many different backgrounds, races, and identities entered her classroom each day. I have personally seen teachers judge students' answers negatively during class discussions, based solely on how that student spoke or appeared. Studies have found negative judgment of students to be common in classrooms, as some teachers have different perceptions of what students were capable, based on different groups of students. Some teachers may see students in a negative way due to their social economic status (Timmermans et al., 2016). Mrs. Johnson did not feed into modern stereotypes placed on certain individuals. Instead, she focused on hearing the variety of answers and ideas from the diverse range of students in her class. Whether a student was asked a closed or open-ended question, she always recognized the validity in each person's answer and thought process. Specifically, I remember a time where I was chosen to discuss a topic in front of the class. In this activity, the class was instructed to move to certain signs hanging around the room. The signs were labeled with the words "agree," "disagree," "strongly agree," "strongly disagree," and "no opinion." Mrs. Johnson read aloud a series of opinions relating to serious topics. The class was instructed to take a side on the opinion. In one instance, I felt strongly about the topic. I moved to the *strongly agree* sign confidently, which my teacher noticed. She called on me, asking me to explain why I strongly agreed. Nervously, I explained. With a smile on her face, she nodded her head and told me I made a valid point and she completely understood why I chose that option.

Choosing someone else to discuss their beliefs, Mrs. Johnson chose a girl who was standing by the *strongly disagree* sign. When she explained her beliefs, Mrs. Johnson nodded, telling the student that she understood her argument and saw the validity in her points as well as mine. In this moment, I felt that I was respected as an individual. Instead of judging me for my beliefs or judging the other student for her beliefs, my teacher chose to respect each of our beliefs and hear what we had to say. In doing this, Mrs. Johnson showed that she respected and accepted what we had to say. In a study by Oldfather (1995), the researcher found that students were very appreciative of having their voices or opinions being heard without judgment. The research also found that students using their voices allowed them to gain confidence and an understanding of what they were capable of (Oldfather, 1995). Allowing students to express their stories, opinions, concerns, or emotions without judgment could help establish students' self-confidence.

Mrs. Johnson believed that all her students had a right to their beliefs or opinions and that those beliefs should be voiced and valued. Just as she encouraged her students to speak their minds, I encourage future and current educators to do the same. If this approach were universally applied, we could create a future generation of individuals who will speak up for what they believe in.

THE BENEFITS OF ESTABLISHING A CARING RELATIONSHIP WITH STUDENTS

In Chapter 1 of *Teacher Educators as Critical Storytellers*, Antonio L. Ellis described his relationship with his music teacher, Mr. McCloud. Ellis stated that he was "encouraged to do just enough to get by academically and in life" (Ellis et al., 2021, p. 7). Similarly, I was this way throughout much of my time in high school. Until Mrs. Johnson, I did not have a teacher who invested in me and made me feel that I was of importance.

Mrs. Johnson, however, was always positive and always displayed happiness, even at 7:30 in the morning. As a student in public school, I arrived at school early. Each morning, I found Mrs. Johnson standing outside her classroom to greet students. Most mornings, she would engage in a conversation with me, asking how I was doing or complimenting the outfit I was wearing. As my years in high school were a difficult time, this action of my teacher always brightened my day and made attending school enjoyable.

Along with other small actions, Mrs. Johnson has also shown endless amounts of kindness to me and her students during the COVID-19 pandemic. Graduating in the year 2020, my in-person high school experience ended abruptly. In March 2020, classes transitioned from in-person attendance to being online only. While this was an upsetting and frustrating time for myself and my graduating class, my English teacher refused to let the pandemic ruin our year. One evening, I arrived at my home after work to find my mom holding a gift for me. I opened the gift to find the book *Oh, the Places You'll Go!* by Dr. Seuss and a keychain with a quote engraved into it. Confused about who the gift was from, my mom told me that my English teacher contacted her and wanted to bring something to me. Opening the book, my teacher had written a heartwarming message. In this message, she expressed her pride in me and how happy she was to have me as a student. During this difficult time, this gesture meant the world to me. It is something I will always remember.

These actions of my teacher showed me that it is easier to be kind than to be hateful to others, especially to those who are going through difficult times. It is understood that

> teachers who show that they genuinely care and make it a point to develop meaningful relationships with their students, irrespective of the environment in which instruction is being delivered, tend to have a positive influence on their students and ultimately on their educational growth. (Hawk & Lyons, 2008, as cited in Kyei-Blankson & Owusu-Ansah, 2016, p. 2)

As Antonio L. Ellis felt encouraged to make Mr. McCloud proud, I feel the same encouragement to do the same for Mrs. Johnson. This teacher had a wonderful impact on me and her other students. She established a caring relationship with each of her students and constantly expressed her belief that each of her students could succeed. I noticed that my peers and I tried our hardest to turn in our best work for this class. Ultimately, the caring words and actions of this teacher allowed for students to find determination to make her proud.

RECOMMENDATIONS FOR CURRENT AND FUTURE EDUCATORS

My favorite English teacher had a positive impact on my life, and the lessons she taught me are ones I will apply as a future educator in my own classroom. I have found the following points to be applicable for both current or future teachers and professors to consider:

- Express pride in students whenever the opportunity arises.
- Allow students to voice their beliefs or concerns within a classroom without negative judgment.
- Establish healthy and sustainable relationships with students. Doing so can create pathways for you to be an influence on the life trajectory of each student.

REFERENCES

Ellis, A. L., Hartlep, N. D., Ladson-Billings, G., & Stovall, D. O. (Eds.). (2021). *Teacher educators as critical storytellers*. Teacher College Press.

Etherington, M. (2019). Pride in education: A narrative study of Finnish school teachers. *SAGE Open, 9*(3). https://doi.org/10.1177%2F2158244019845489

Hawk, T. F., & Lyons, P. R. (2008). Please don't give up on me: When faculty fail to care. *Journal of Management Education, 32*(3), 316–338. https://doi.org/10.1177/1052562908314194

Kyei-Blankson, L., & Owusu-Ansah, A. (2016). Going back to the basics: Demonstrating care, connectedness, and a pedagogy of relationship in education. *World Journal of Education, 6*(3), 1–9. https://doi.org/10.5430/wje.v6n3p1

Oldfather, P. (1995). Songs "come back most to them": Students' experiences as researchers. *Theory Into Practice, 34*(2), 131–137. http://www.jstor.org/stable/1476962

Timmermans, A. C., De Boer, H., & Van der Werf, M. P. C. (2016). An investigation of the relationship between teachers' perceptions of student attributes. *Social Psychology of Education, 19*, 217–240. https://doi.org/10.1007/s11218-015-9326-6

CHAPTER 16

THE PRESENCE OF MS. MILLER

Teacher as a Caregiver

Britney Conner

High school was a very rough time for me. I slacked on my grades, had trouble making friends, and had a rough home life. I attended school every day just to avoid the consequences of being at home, but also for the excitement of learning something new. Throughout my life, I was in and out of foster care, and I constantly relocated to different houses with different families. That was, until I found my final home. Even though it was the last place I lived, it was still rough living there. Having crippling anxiety and mental health problems, I found it hard to make friends. Then one day, I volunteered to work in the guidance office. My job was to file papers and bring passes to students so they could meet with their counselor, meanwhile making sure I could get my work done at the same time. While working there, I developed a close relationship with the guidance secretary, Ms. Miller. She was the sweetest lady, with big brown eyes. At first, I was not sure if we would get along, but after a while I knew that she was placed in my life for a reason.

Lift Every Voice, pages 81–83
Copyright © 2024 by Information Age Publishing
www.infoagepub.com
All rights of reproduction in any form reserved.

Every day when I came into the office, Ms. Miller always asked how I was doing and for updates on my life. As a faculty member, she made me feel so included, she was almost like my best friend. Despite our age difference, Ms. Miller and I just "clicked." She inspired me to keep pushing through life and fight to get through school to be the person I wanted to be.

No one else in my family ever made it past high school. They either worked in lower-paying jobs or remained unemployed. I knew I did not want to take that route, and so did Ms. Miller. She is the reason why I applied for admission at Radford University. She made me feel like I had a chance to achieve success in life. She believed in me far more than I believed in myself.

Because of my family history, I had a very narrow, limited vision about what I could become in life. At times when life felt unmanageable, Ms. Miller constantly encouraged me. In most situations, Ms. Miller was the only stable support I had at school. I remember getting lunch from the cafeteria and eating with her every day while chatting about classes and the upcoming school year, which included my goals for the future. She was always supportive and attentive to what I conveyed. While she enjoyed talking about the importance of an education and my aspirations, she also showed her full humanity. We often made inside jokes. We showed each other pictures of our family.

Furthermore, Ms. Miller always did things that would benefit me, like packing extra snacks in her office so I always had something to eat. She brought me lightly used clothing so that I would be able to dress appropriately for job interviews. She always supported me. There were times I felt overwhelmed, I would go to her office sobbing, and she would be there to support me.

After I graduated, we exchanged contact information and agreed to communicate often. I invited Ms. Miller to my graduation party. She gave me large bags of items I needed for college. Ms. Miller texted me Bible verses every day for 2 years.

My heart was especially touched in 2021 when my biological mother passed away. My family could not afford a funeral service, because my mother was not employed and my family was financially constrained. However, we created a GoFundMe page and campaign to raise money for my mother's cremation. Ms. Miller was the first person to make a donation. Even though I did not ask, she did it because she knew it meant a lot to me.

I will never forget all Ms. Miller did for me academically, financially, and emotionally. Recently, I was able to reconnect with her. We caught up with one another and she offered to help me purchase items for my apartment next year.

However, what inspired me the most is when she mentioned how big an impact I had made on her life! She told me she believes God put me in her life for a reason beyond her human comprehension. She inspired me to be a first-generation college student who attends college and plans to graduate. She had faith in me when no one else did. I will forever be grateful for her friendship and commitment to helping me.

CHAPTER 17

HOW TEACHERS HAVE AFFECTED ME

Jacob Mays

I did not notice the impact teachers had on my life until I looked back retrospectively. Some teachers I did not have any connection with, others a negative connection with, and some a positive connection. I found enough positive connections to do well, but how could I and my teachers have made all our connections positive entirely? How many students in education do not have a positive relationship with any teachers?

I have been taught by over 50 teachers in K–12 schools, but only a few of those experiences are notable as being positive. The best teachers are those who are supportive, encouraging, respectful, open, knowledgeable, understanding, and caring. A good teacher will implement many teaching methods and support students who have differing strengths. Some students may work well by themselves, in small groups, or in large groups. Finding a way for all students to have equal opportunities to succeed is key to keeping students active in the classroom. The classroom environment should allow students to be divergent thinkers. Often teachers will discipline students if they do not produce academically or model behaviors that are expected at school. For example, I was very good at math in middle school. In sixth grade I moved up from the standard math class to Pre-AP because I had over a 100% average. However, my grades began plummeting in math in seventh and eighth grades, because I found alternative ways to do my math while still producing the right answer. However, because I was not using the formula taught in class, my answers were marked incorrect. This unjust grading system made me move away from math and lose confidence in my math abilities. In high school I continued to perform poorly in math but excelled in other subjects.

I believe educators should encourage and admire students' finding their own way to excel and succeed. I will now dive further into teachers who developed positive and negative relationships with me, without naming their names out of respect for their privacy.

The teacher I had the most positive connection with and learned a lot from tried to connect with students on a personal level. He would often sit at desks with us when we were in groups, making class feel more like a conversation than a lecture. It almost seemed as if he was on the same level with us because he sat amid students, while still maintaining our respect as our teacher in the classroom. This educator also found a good balance of not doing a task or assignment for too long. He believed that younger students do better when activities are roughly thirty minutes or less. Any longer, he believed, was not a good use of time. He kept the class interesting by rotating to other ways to learn the course material, whether it was writing notes during his lecture, doing worksheets on our own, having group discussions and group projects, playing games in groups to answer questions as in Jeopardy or Kahoot, and lastly, watching videos to aid students visually with the material. Like most good teachers, this teacher used varied teaching methods to keep students interested. If some students do not perform well or like one task, the next one will probably suit their needs better. This teacher didn't leave anyone out or view some of us as inferior; he saw potential in every one of us. In my opinion, that is the most important characteristic of a teacher.

Unfortunately, I have also experienced a teacher who made me feel small. In my theater arts class during my junior and senior years in high school, the teacher simply disliked me, and it was quite evident. I was in class with my best friend, and we were both very respectful and present in class, actively participating in theater activities. My friend and I played main characters in the play *The Crucible*, and I believe we performed well. However, for whatever reason, the teacher seemed to love my friend but did not like me. It may have been because my older brother was in his class years before me and was also in various plays. Maybe the teacher compared me to my brother in negative ways.

My friend and I performed well in the play and in class roles, but when we got report cards, under the teachers notes, the teacher would put negative comments for me and positive comments for my friend. I also believe he graded my assignments harder. This was very unfair in my eyes, but I didn't see a way of fixing it. It was clear the teacher picked favorites. When I auditioned for a play the next year, he did not cast me, after taking advice from a student he made co-director, who happened to be someone who had a grudge against me. My friend did not audition for this play, but we both returned later to host the talent show shortly before we graduated.

I really enjoyed acting in theater and being on stage, but this teacher's personal feelings towards me held me back from pursuing the art. This kind of negativity is one of the worst things a teacher can do to a student. There is a difference between pushing students with tough love to reach their potential, compared to blatantly disliking some students to the point that the teacher's attitude affects students' grades, mental health, and interests. Good teachers try to see the best in their students, even though in rare instances, they may have valid reasons for disliking a student. Nevertheless, they should try their best to set aside those feelings for the benefit of the student. For example, maybe my theater teacher should have held blind auditions or have the name of assignments on the back of papers as a way to keep bias out of the process. In conclusion, educators must accept that they will have students with different upbringings, races and ethnicities, nationalities, genders, political views, religions, and household lifestyles. A good teacher acknowledges all forms of diversity and models respect for all students. All it takes is one teacher to believe in a child. Every child deserves to have that kind of teacher.

CHAPTER 18

MRS. OWENS AND MS. C

A Comparative Analysis of Two Teachers

Kelcie Lemons

I have had some phenomenal teachers throughout my schooling experience. The public school system I was a part of hired teachers carefully and valued students' feedback. I never had any issues with a teacher except for one, who later was terminated. In this chapter I will briefly share my experiences with two high school teachers, one excellent and one far below the ideal.

Mrs. Candace Owens, my 11th grade AP English teacher, was an amazing teacher who left a lasting impact on my life. Her positive influence is why I decided to attend Radford University. She graduated from Radford University with a Bachelor of Science in English and a Master of Arts in literature.

Mrs. Owens quickly became more than just a teacher to her students. She treated students like family. She was our counselor, mentor, biggest supporter, and overall inspiration. Students referred to her as their "school mom." She had no biological children, but she had motherly instincts her students enjoyed.

I never had a teacher who went above and beyond for students, until I met Mrs. Owens. She went out of her way every day to show how much she cared for us. She pushed all of us to do our best, and she did not believe in failure. Ms. Owens made all students aware of their capabilities and pushed them to be the best version of themselves. She responded to students within 24 hours and was always willing to help with assignments, even those that were not for her class.

Mrs. Owens also knew how to make everyone's day brighter. She would often surprise the class with snacks and treats, and she planned fun activities to give us a break from schoolwork. She also showed us memes every day at the beginning of class, to start the day with a laugh. The researchers Yeager and Walton (2011) found that "small" social-psychological interventions that focus on changing students' thoughts, feelings, and beliefs in and about school can lead to large gains in student achievement for each and every student.

"Improving students' relationships with teachers has important, positive and long-lasting implications for both students' academic and social development," stated Rimm-Kaufman and Sandilos (2015, p. 1). In my view, Mrs. Owens' upbeat, creative touches made school more enjoyable and changed my whole attitude towards high school. I personally feel as if her teaching style is something everyone should use.

Sadly, my 11th grade year is when the COVID-19 pandemic started, and Ms. Owens' class got cut short by two months when our school closed and we switched to online classes. I will never forget when the rumors of school closing went around, and everyone thought it was a joke. Ms. Owens planned a "school break" party for us when they announced we would be out for two weeks. Students were so excited to get a break from school.

We got to come back to school for a short period after the two weeks, only to be told we would be finishing the rest of the semester virtually. Students were in shock about the whole situation, and our happiness at having a break instantly turned into misery.

Although we never got to be together in the classroom again, our class still remained a family. A month after we had been doing virtual school, Ms. Owens sent everyone positive letters encouraging our success. We had a group chat, and our class remained in contact. Mrs. Owens recently planned a class reunion for us. Reuniting made my heart full. Her taking the time out of her life to plan a reunion is just one example of how she went out of her way to show her students how much she valued them. Ms. Owens is truly a phenomenal individual who proved how much she cared for and valued students.

She cared for students so much that she continued supporting us when we were no longer her students. During the first semester of my senior year, school was completely virtual. A new teacher came to teach virtually; I will call her Ms. C. She was very unpleasant, and she seemed as if she was out to get us all. She was also an English teacher like Mrs. Owens; however, Ms. C. and Mrs. Owens were like day and night—complete opposites.

Ms. C gave us overwhelming amounts of assignments and told us we should spend 9 hours focusing on her class per week. She accused students of cheating in her class because we successfully completed assignments. Seemingly, she expected us to fail. She attempted to put many students on academic probation and tried to ruin our future educational aspirations.

Fortunately, we had Mrs. Owens to advocate for us. Ms. Owens knew that we studied faithfully in order to achieve academic success. She had a private meeting with Ms. C. and attempted to address the concerns students were raising. Unfortunately, Ms. C. disregarded Ms. Owens. Therefore, some students escalated their concerns to the school principal.

The principal was a very kind and loving man. He showed care for all of his students and valued their opinions. Once he found out about Ms. C.'s behavior, he began to monitor how much work she assigned. He set up Zoom meetings with our class to check in and ensure she was not being too harsh on us. Still, Ms. C. continued to assign a level of work that was unachievable, resulting in her being terminated.

If not for Ms. Owens, we might have been stuck with Ms. C. and potentially failed her class. I am so thankful for Mrs. Owens and the compassion she showed us. I feel Mrs. Owens was both a teacher and counselor combined. Students paid close attention in her class because everyone had such great respect for her. As a result of her belief in her students, everyone excelled.

All students need someone to advocate for and motivate them, just as Ms. Owens did for us. In a popular Ted Talk aired by the Public Broadcasting Service (PBS) and frequently viewed on YouTube, educator Rita Pierson said, "Every child deserves a champion—an adult who will never give up on them, who understands the power of connection and insists that they become the best that they can possibly be."

Mrs. Owens was our champion.

REFERENCES

Rimm-Kaufman, S., & Sandilos, L. (2015). Improving students' relationships with teachers to provide essential supports for learning. *Applications of Psychological Science to Teaching and Learning Modules.* American Psychological Association. https://www.apa.org/education-career/k12/relationships

Yeager, D. S., & Walton, G. M. (2011). Social-psychological interventions in education. *Review of Educational Research, 81*(2), 267–301. https://doi.org/10.3102/0034654311405999

AFTERWORD

EMBRACING THE POWER OF STUDENT VOICES IN TEACHER EDUCATION

Antonio L. Ellis

In the pages of *Lift Every Voice: Radford University Teacher Education Students*, we encounter a chorus of voices, each one resonating with the authenticity and wisdom of lived experience. As their former professor, I am profoundly moved by the courage and vulnerability displayed by our undergraduate contributors. Through their narratives, they assert their rightful place as emerging authorities in the realm of teacher education, challenging traditional notions of expertise and knowledge dissemination. By employing a critical storytelling methodology, these students illuminate the profound impact of classroom practices on their academic, social, and emotional development.

At the heart of this volume lies a powerful assertion: that the voices and life experiences of undergraduate teacher education students deserve recognition, validation, and legitimacy within the broader discourse of teacher preparation. By amplifying these voices, we not only enrich our understanding of the complexities of teaching and learning but also empower future educators to critically examine their own practices and assumptions. The stories, anecdotes, and analyses contained within these pages offer invaluable insights and lessons that have the potential to transform the way we approach teacher education.

One of the most striking aspects of this volume is the resilience and agency demonstrated by our student contributors. Despite facing myriad challenges and obstacles, they refuse to be passive recipients of education; instead, they actively engage with and interrogate the systems and structures that shape their experiences. In doing so, they not only reclaim their own narratives but also inspire others to do the same. Their stories serve as a powerful reminder of the transformative potential of education to uplift, empower, and liberate individuals and communities. As the visionary of this volume, I hope that *Lift Every Voice* will serve as a catalyst for dialogue, reflection, and action within the field of teacher education. I envision this volume as a resource for preservice and classroom teachers who are committed to creating more inclusive, equitable, and culturally responsive learning environments. The stories shared by our student contributors offer valuable lessons and insights that can inform and enrich the practice of educators at all levels.

Lift Every Voice underscores the importance of centering student voices and experiences in the ongoing conversation about educational reform and transformation. Too often, the perspectives of those directly impacted by educational policies and practices are overlooked or marginalized. This volume challenges us to listen to and learn from the voices of undergraduate teacher education students, recognizing them as invaluable partners in the quest for educational equity and justice. In closing, I extend my deepest gratitude to our student contributors for their courage, vulnerability, and authenticity. I also thank our readers for engaging with these narratives with an open mind and heart. May the stories contained within *Lift Every Voice* serve as a source of inspiration, reflection, and empowerment for all who are committed to the transformative power of education. Together, let us lift every voice in the pursuit of a more just, equitable, and inclusive future for all learners.

ABOUT THE EDITORS

Antonio L. Ellis is a senior professorial lecturer and director of the Institute on Education Equity and Justice at the American University School of Education. He teaches special education courses and advises students in the educational leadership and policy doctoral program.

Lisa Maria Grillo currently serves as the president of Seton High School and instructor in the Department of Educational Leadership and Policy Studies in the Howard University School of Education. Her research is currently focused on the experiences of Black and Latina women who lead in educational settings. Prior to this role, Lisa successfully led district and school level initiatives to improve student outcomes for diverse student populations in large urban and suburban school districts.

Jania Hutchinson is a graduating senior in the Radford University School of Teacher Education and Leadership. She is passionate about educating all populations of children. Jania was the first Teachers of Tomorrow cadet to pass all three portions of the Praxis Core exam. She accredits much of her academic success to her former teacher, Ms. Eddy Janney. Jania is a resident of Roanoke, Virginia.

ABOUT THE CONTRIBUTORS

Victoria Branscome is a graduating senior in the Radford University School of Teacher Education and Leadership. Victoria is a resident of Troutville, Virginia.

Allison G. Brown is a graduating senior in the Radford University School of Teacher Education and Leadership. Allison is a resident of Radford, Virginia.

Britney Conner is a graduating senior in the Radford University School of Teacher Education and Leadership. Britney is a resident of Radford, Virginia.

Kaylee Golder is a junior special education major at Radford University. Kaylee is a native of Botetourt, Virginia.

Joleigh Helton is a senior elementary education major at Radford University. Joleigh is a native of Boones Mill, Virginia.

Madison F. Keaton is a graduating senior in the Radford University School of Teacher Education and Leadership. Madison is a resident of Narrows, Virginia.

Brooke E. Kelly is a graduating senior in the Radford University School of Teacher Education and Leadership. Brooke is a resident of Radford, Virginia.

Kelcie Lemons is a graduating senior at Radford University with a major in communication sciences and disorders, and a minor in special education.

98 • About the Contributors

Kelcie will be attending graduate school at Radford University to become a speech-language pathologist. Kelcie is a native of Ridgeway, Virginia.

Jacob Mays is a graduating senior in the Radford University School of Teacher Education and Leadership. Jacob is a resident of Radford, Virginia.

Claire Morris is a graduating senior in the Radford University School of Teacher Education and Leadership. Claire is a resident of Salem, Virginia.

Maddison (Maddie) Parrish is a senior special education and psychology major at Radford University. Maddie is a native of Salem, Virginia.

Taylor Poff is a graduating senior in the Radford University School of Teacher Education and Leadership. Taylor is a resident of Radford, Virginia.

Jenna Staton is a graduating senior in the Radford University School of Teacher Education and Leadership. Jenna is a resident of Salem, Virginia.

Jada Turner is a graduating senior in the Radford University School of Teacher Education and Leadership. Jada is a resident of Radford, Virginia.

Katherine Wagoner is a graduating senior in the Radford University School of Teacher Education and Leadership. Katherine is a resident of Radford, Virginia.

Jabin Walker is a graduating senior at Radford University. His major is exercise, sport, and health education. He is a member of Alpha Phi Alpha Fraternity, Incorporated. Jabin is a native of South Hill, Virginia.

Shyheim Woods is a graduating senior in the Radford University School of Teacher Education and Leadership. Shyheim is a resident of Bassett, Virginia.

Christian R. Worley is a graduating senior psychology major at Radford University. Christian is a native of Big Stone Gap, VA.